Leisureguy's

Guide to Gourmet Shaving
Shaving Made Enjoyable

Second Edition

By
Michael Ham
'LeisureGuy'

Pogonotomy Press
Monterey California

Copyright © 2007, 2008 by Michael Ham
All rights reserved.

Edition 2.03 – August 2008
ISBN 978-1-4303-2807-0
Book available at www.lulu.com/leisureguy

To AM, who insisted that I write it
To EH, who might find it useful
To GM and CM, who someday will read it
To KV, for the phrase "gourmet shaving"
To K★, for taking up wetshaving
And, of course, to The Wife, for listening to all these
discoveries with exemplary forbearance.

Contents

Preface to the Second Edition

T HINGS have changed since the first edition was published. I have continued to experiment and to learn, and new vendors and products have emerged. Thus, it seemed a good idea to revise and expand (primarily expand) the first edition to reflect what I now know.

Traditional wet shaving (with a double-edged blade, safety razor, shaving brush, and shaving cream or shaving soap) seems to be on the increase. Some indications:

- A constant stream of new traditional shavers joining the shaving forums for advice and instruction.
- New vendors of traditional shaving products coming on-line and enjoying success.
- New traditional safety razors being introduced (for example, the Merkur 38C and the slant version of that razor).
- The prices of vintage safety razors on eBay increasing.

All this shows a growing demand and a growing market as men abandon expensive and marketing-driven shaving tools for the pleasures of traditional shaving.

I hope you'll join us.

Michael Ham
Leisureguy.wordpress@gmail.com

Preface

FOR most men, shaving is a daily yet unappealing task: a routine at best, a chore more often. And a surprising number of men believe that they have "sensitive skin," because the tug-and-cut action of the common multiblade shaving cartridge and the pressure they exert on the razor trying to get a close shave, together with inadequate beard preparation from a pressurized can of shaving mix, gives them skin irritation, razor burn, razor bumps, and in-grown hairs.

It's all completely avoidable: the daily shaving task can easily be transformed into a pleasurable ritual that leaves the shaver feeling renewed and pampered and his skin glowing with health. All it takes are the right tools, the right preparation, and a little practice.

This book introduces the shaver to the world of traditional wetshaving: the badger brush and exquisitely formulated shaving soaps and creams and the well-designed safety razor—still readily available and even in current manufacture—that uses a double-edged blade to provide a perfect shave.

And high-quality double-edged blades, available for as little as 9¢ a blade, will last most shavers the same amount of time as a $3.50 disposable multiblade shaving cartridge, while providing a better shave—better both in quality and in enjoyment.

The learning curve is short, and the enjoyment is immense, so get started today.

ONE

What this is

T HIS book is for men who shave without enjoyment or who are just learning to shave. It describes a method of shaving that transforms a daily chore into a pleasurable ritual. It's a beginner's guide to wetshaving: how to shave with a safety razor and not hurt yourself. (A safety razor uses a double-edged blade and is often called a "DE razor.")

Shaving with a safety razor and using a shaving brush and high-quality shaving cream or soap for lather has several benefits:

- The shave itself is enjoyable and satisfying
- Your skin feels better because the double-edged blade cuts the whiskers cleanly, unlike the "tug-and-cut" action of the multiblade disposable cartridge.
- The cost of shaving is substantially less. Double-edged blades cost pennies and are normally good for 4-6 shaves; a puck of shaving soap or tub of shaving cream lasts for months.
- You get a smoother, closer shave without irritating your skin.

This guide takes you step by step through the whole process. It discusses in detail the equipment and supplies you need and where to get them. It describes how to prepare your beard for a shave and the basic techniques in building a good lather and using the razor. It provides guidance for dealing with common problems like acne and razor bumps. And it points to on-line sources of more information that can help you address any particular problems you might encounter.

My goal: to create a useful and comprehensive reference for the novice safety-razor shaver. Based on the feedback and comments I've received, that goal has been achieved.

A word on the Web links in the book: The Web is home to a vast profusion of information about almost any topic, with shaving no exception. In no way could I include in this book all the information—much of it useful—that you can find on the Web. But, I realized, I can provide *links* to some of that information.

So my approach to writing the book was to include in the book all the essential information to take you into the pleasures of shaving with brush and soap and safety razor—and also to provide links to ancillary information that you may find interesting and/or useful. My suggestion is that you simply read the book, reserving the links for later, and only for those things that you want to explore further.

To improve the readability of the text—and because I suggest that you initially simply read the book, not look up all the links—I've placed the links in endnotes following the Appendix. And, to make the links even easier to use, I've also provided them on the Web as hyperlinks so that you can simply click one to go to the site of interest.

The Web list of links is especially worth checking since I update it as new information becomes available—for example, price changes that affect recommendations, or I learn of a new vendor. See **http://tinyurl.com/4rt6nf** for the list of clickable links on the Web. I recommend that you bookmark that page.

TWO

Who I am

I began shaving (with a Gillette DE safety razor) around 1955. After a couple of years I switched to a Schick Injector, a safety razor that uses a single-edged blade. But that was then, in the dark ages of the isolated shaver, when each shaver had to depend on his own knowledge and what he could pick up from members of his family.

The only sources of information I had, for example, were my step-dad (who knew no more than I about shaving) and commercials and ads, whose general content was, "Buy this product." I used Old Spice shaving soap and built the lather directly in the soap mug. I used Gillette Blue Blades, and my shave consisted of two complete passes: one down, and one up—the second with no lather. I used little pieces of toilet paper on the resulting nicks and over the course of my high-school career must have used up several rolls. As soon as I got to college, I grew a beard.

I still remember reading in high school a near-future science-fiction novel about a guy getting ready for a big night. He lathers up and shaves with the grain, then he lathers up *again* and shaves against the grain. I thought, "That's odd—he lathered up a *second* time." It never occurred to me that this might be the right way to shave.

Today—now—is truly the golden age of shaving. Only with the Internet has it been possible for the far-flung band of safety-razor shavers to pool the knowledge gained from their experience and trials and provide all shavers, new or old, with so much information, and to provide easy global access to vendors of wet-shaving products.

This book grew out of my own experience, augmented and illuminated by the experience of other shavers in the shaving forums, and I thank all the guys on ShaveMyFace.com, TheShaveDen.com, the

RazorandBrush.com Message Board, and BadgerandBlade.com. I also thank the vendors listed in the appendix for the fine array of products they offer, which are essential to the practice of traditional shaving.

I hope that you enjoy your journey of exploration.

THREE

Why to do it

BEFORE we start, I should answer this question: "Why bother?" Or, as a friend put it, why put aside all the modern technology of pressurized cans of formulated shaving foams and gels and the modern multiblade razor cartridge that allows you to shave while still half asleep? Why pick up tools and techniques from a generation (or two) ago? Those who have made the switch offer these answers:

Care of skin

For some, the reason is pragmatic and down-to-earth: the multiblade cartridge uses a tug-and-cut technique that, along with the dry chemical lather squirted from a pressurized can, leads to ingrown whiskers, razor bumps, and skin irritation for many shavers, most of whom think that they have "sensitive skin." They continue to suffer, buying loads of products promoted as protective pre-shaves and as soothing and healing aftershave treatments in hopes of repairing the damage. Some, however, switch to the double-edged blade and safety razor for the comfort they achieve with single-blade shaving. Most find that, once they master the techniques and skills of traditional shaving, their skin problems vanish.

A guy in one of the shaving forums commented that he started traditional shaving and, after a few months, returned home to see his mom. She felt his cheek and commented that it was the smoothest and softest it had been since he was 5. He said he had been aware that traditional shaving had improved his skin, but the improvement was so gradual he really didn't understand how dramatic the change was.[1]

Quality of shave

Some men choose a safety razor with a double-edged blade because they enjoy getting a much better shave: smoother, closer, and longer-lasting. This contradicts the ads about the latest disposable multiblade cartridges, but ads—brace yourself—frequently stretch the truth.

Cost of shave

Today, one Gillette Fusion disposable multiblade cartridge costs $3.50. One double-edged blade, which will last you roughly as many shaves as the cartridge, costs as little as 9-12¢. In addition, a puck of shaving soap—say, one from Honeybee Spa—costs $3.79 and in daily use will last around 3 months. The razor and the brush last a lifetime—indeed, even longer: some shavers enjoy using double-edged razors from 80 years ago. Even one Sensor twin-blade disposable cartridge now costs around $1.60. You can buy a complete safety razor kit for a beginner—razor, 5 blades of each of 5 different brands (25 blades total), brush, and soap—for the price of 10 Fusion cartridges.

Quality of life

I didn't have skin problems and wasn't all that unhappy with the shaves the Mach 3 delivered. I turned to safety-razor shaving for the sheer pleasure the morning shave now affords. Shaving has changed from a routine at best, a chore more often, to a wonderful ritual from which I emerge feeling truly pampered. I now *look forward* to shaving each day. That feeling more than repays the little bit of equipment required. The daily shave: a daily pleasure. How many can say that?

Very few. I strongly suspect that the current fashion of young men wearing a stubble of 4 or 5 days' growth has its origin in how unpleasant shaving is for most men who use today's shaving paraphernalia. Fashion photographers, seeing many young men going unshaven with visible stubble, decided it was a "look," and put such men in ads, trying to appeal to that demographic. In fact, these young men simply don't like to shave but for whatever reason may not grow a full beard. So they put off shaving, and the look becomes a fashion statement and provides the Significant Other with a sandpaper experience along with every kiss.

Those who use traditional equipment, in sharp contrast, enjoy shaving. In fact, I found that the focused attention and meditative mindset of shaving with a safety razor can provide a Zen experience in the morning shave, a ritual not unlike the tea ceremony:

Special room – check
Special mode of dress – check
Contemplative, unrushed mindset – check
Cleanliness and order – check
Practice of technique requires focused attention (aka flow) – check
Use of special tools, often old – check
Tools both functional and aesthetically pleasing – check
Suspension of mind chatter, critical judgments – check
Senses—sight, hearing, touch, smell—fully engaged – check
Physical enjoyment of sources of warmth – check
Awareness & enjoyment of aromas arising from hot water – check
Definite sequence of steps – check
Structure of the entire experience repeated each time – check
Feeling of pleasure, fulfillment, and satisfaction at end – check

Flow[2] is the state of mind that results when one loses consciousness of self and of time, being totally focused on a task whose intricacy and difficulty require about 85% of one's capacity. (If the task is too easy, attention wanders; if it's too difficult, anxiety results.)

Most people know that happiness is a state generally recognized only after the fact—at the time, while happy, one is not aware of it *per se*, but simply enjoys each moment. Flow, as it turns out, seems to exactly describe that state, so the more flow one can arrange, the happier one's life. Shaving, with the right approach and mindset and attention, can promote flow.

The contemplative aspect of a satisfying shaving ritual is important. Most of us live hurried lives, multitasking and rushing about, harried by time demands. What the morning shave with a safety razor offers is a small oasis of unhurried calm and single-minded attention to remind you what it feels like to be unrushed and not to be doing one thing while thinking of something else.

And if modern psychology is to be believed, it even seems possible that this shaving ritual can increase your self-esteem: Cognitive dissonance[3] posits that a person holding contradictory beliefs (or observing himself acting in contradiction to his beliefs) will add to or modify his beliefs to resolve or reduce the contradiction[4].

I thought of this regarding shaving (of course): By acquiring the specialized tools and supplies and taking the time and care to create a shaving ritual, the shaver presents himself with a behavior that leads to increased self-esteem: "If I'm taking this much time to pamper myself, I must be worth it." Not a bad feeling at all.

A summary of reasons men enjoy traditional shaving:

Sensual enjoyment: hot lather, the feel of a flexible yet firm shaving brush, the razor making a nice sound as it mows through the stubble, feeling your smooth face after the shave, the fragrances of the lather and the aftershave, etc.

Flow: as described above: focused attention on a task that requires around 85% of your capabilities, with a clear goal and immediate feedback as you work at it. It really clears the mind.

Gadget appeal: brush styles, razor mechanisms, blade characteristics, soap varieties, etc.

The great feeling of **transforming a daily chore into a daily pleasure**: conquering, in a small way, drudgery itself.

Frugality: the satisfaction of knowing that soap and blade cost just pennies, rather than the high-priced products of marketing that other men typically use.

Finally, **getting the best (smoothest, closest) shaves of your life** with zero skin irritation.

If it's so great, why are cartridges so popular?

Some guys are skeptical because "everyone" uses cartridges. So why was the double-edged blade abandoned? The answer will shock you: money.

In the 1950's Personna (GEM/Ever-Ready etc) invented the Stainless Steel Blade and marketed them for their single edge razors. The blades were sharper but they found that the edge deteriorated quickly and became quite rough to shave with.

Wilkinson Sword was in the forefront with the technology to coat the edge with Platinum, Chromium, PTFE (Teflon), etc., for a smoother shave. Wilkinson held many of the patents and grabbed a considerable proportion of Gillette's market share ever so quickly in the late 50's early 60's — basically, WS blades were noticeably better. And so Gillette made a deal for them to use Wilkinson technology. All of this helped in the demise of the DE as Gillette's patents were coming to an end and they were no longer in the controlling seat. Gillette decided to take a new direction in the early 1960's and cartridge systems would be the end result.[5]

The Fear Barrier

Some have expressed a fear of the safety razor; to those I point out that it's called a *safety* razor for a reason: the only damage you might encounter are some few nicks while you're learning (as compared to years of skin irritation and other problems stemming from use of the multiblade cartridge). Very quickly your technique improves so that any start-up problems vanish.

Indeed, you can begin by continuing to use your multiblade cartridge razor and just adding to your routine a fragrant lather you create with a badger brush and a high-quality shaving cream or shaving soap—much more satisfying than squirting some goop from a can of shaving mix. And then perhaps you might move to a Schick injector razor (described later), which has a feel very like a cartridge razor and is easy to shave with.

Sooner or later, though, you will probably want to try a safety razor: a great shave with a blade that costs less than 5% of the cost of one Gillette Fusion disposable cartridge.

If you want, you can use a practice blade to perfect your technique before using a real blade: cut a piece of thin stiff plastic to blade size and use it in your razor to practice using very light pressure and the correct blade angle (shallow, almost parallel to the skin).

In a way, the fear that precedes your first shave with a safety razor resembles the similar fear that precedes your first kiss with someone on whom you have a great crush. Your mind is filled with everything that can go wrong, but you decide to try it anyway, and you get a kiss in return—and suddenly everything is okay. The fears are revealed to be but phantasms, and they vanish in the pleasure of the experience. Don't just take my word for it: give it a go.

One safety-razor shaver pointed out that, if you were to describe a cartridge razor to someone in the old days, it would sound quite scary: "*Five* blades?! Won't you cut yourself a lot?" The fear of the safety razor may be merely the fear of a new experience, a distaste for feeling awkward while you acquire new skills.

You also might want to read the following report[6] from someone who's grown accustomed to the safety razor:

> Last weekend I went home. My uncertainty about whether to check or carry on was solved by forgetting to pack my Futur [razor] (I was going to decide when I left work whether to leave it in the bag). So my only real shaving option were the things that I had left at home. I wasn't about to drag out the old Norelco, so that meant the Mach3 that I left there as a spare.
>
> I have not tried a Mach3 a single time since picking up a DE, so I was actually very curious how it would go. I had often wondered if it was really that much different. After all, unlike some, I remember getting decent shaves with it. But then, I never went against the grain, so my shaves were not that smooth. I did use shaving soap and a brush.
>
> First impression is that this thing does not sit well in the hand. I remembered the metal handle having decent weight, but, well, by comparison [with the Futur] the Mach 3 felt dinky. Also much too light in the head.
>
> With the grain. Ugh. Maybe good soap is not as compatible/does not protect as well when using a cartridge? It felt REALLY scratchy. Not tearing up my face or anything, just not pleasant. Much to my surprise, I realized that even with three blades, the one-pass N–S result was not as good as I can get with many DE combinations. So I decided to keep going, and see if my improved technique and good soap would allow a good multipass shave.
>
> I did three passes, but never fully against the grain because I was getting too much irritation going across. With a Feather DE

blade in any decent razor, this would have left me with a near BBS [baby-bottom smooth] shave. With the M3 it was good, but not great. But the real problem was irritation. My skin simply did not look happy. And sure enough, there came the red bumps.

I had to back down to a one pass with the grain the next day, and the third day just did not shave at all.

So, the conclusion is that a DE really does get me a MUCH better result, both in closeness and comfort. What is interesting about this, though, is that this is coming from someone who was perfectly happy with his Mach3 and saw no need to change. I only tried a DE because of the price of stupid cartridges, and the guy love of gadgets.

And, more recently, this note, under the title "What was I thinking?"[7]:

I've just returned from a week in DC. Given that I have a few Mach 3 blades lying around, I decided to take these instead of my DE. Not only that, but I used a can of Nivea shaving foam. It's been some time since I used a combo like this, and my face didn't thank me one little bit!! It's taken a week of using my usual combo (Progress [razor], Trumper [shaving cream], and Rooney [brush]) to calm my face down and get rid of the ingrown hairs. Needless to say, none of the offending items accompanied me on the flight home and all my remaining Mach3 blades have been sent off to a good home. Don't think I'll make that mistake again…

On a positive note, it has made me appreciate more the whole shaving 'experience'.

FOUR

What to expect

B ASED on what many shavers have experienced, you can expect something like the following.

You initially feel skeptical of the idea, but that's followed by the thought that the way you shave now is a chore and your skin is in terrible shape. So, you think, why not give it a shot?

You order a razor, either from an on-line vendor (see Appendix) or on eBay[8] or through the Selling/Trading section of one of the shaving forums. You go to the drugstore and get a cheap brush and shaving soap. You buy any convenient double-edged blade—because the blade is so cheap, it doesn't seem all that important.

You lather up and—very carefully—pull the razor down your cheek. You try to remember what you've read about the correct angle, and you try to exert very little pressure. (Light pressure is particularly difficult for cartridge shavers to learn, who have been using firm pressure to try to get a close shave.)

You finish, perhaps with a nick (but maybe not: the first shave is done *very* carefully) and—on the whole—not bad. In fact, it was sort of interesting.

You decide to check in at the shaving forums—to read more and also perhaps to brag a little. So you go to ShaveMyFace.com and/or TheShaveDen.com and/or BadgerandBlade.com. You post the results of your experience, and you start reading.

You suddenly realize you've spent more than an hour reading messages in the forum, and you now understand quite a bit more about the process, including some ways to improve your technique.

You order a blade sampler pack (the largest one from RazorandBrush.com) so that you have a large number of different blades to try in addition to all the blades you can find locally in the drugstore, and you stop by a Crabtree & Evelyn store to get a better brush and perhaps pick up a shaving cream.

Within a week of your first shave with the safety razor, your shaves are getting progressively better and the nicks have become rare. If you do get a nick, you check pressure and blade angle and resume.

When you encounter a problem or difficulty, you post a question in one of the shaving forums (ShaveMyFace.com, TheShaveDen.com, or BadgerandBlade.com) or on the RazorandBrush.com message board. You usually get advice from someone who had the identical problem and figured out a solution.

You start to really get the hang of it. You've spent some time reading the forum and eyeing the various choices of razors, brushes, soaps, creams, and aftershaves. You're working your way through the sampler pack, and already you can tell that the blades are doing a better job—or maybe your technique is improving—or both.

You are learning so much, and it's so interesting—fascinating, even—that you are eagerly tell your significant other all about it. You observe a certain amount of rolling of the eyes, whatever that means.

Now, as you read the forums, you occasionally find a question from a newbie that you can answer.

One day, after a couple of weeks, you feel your face after shaving and realize that it's smooth—and not just "smooth," but baby-bottom smooth! In every direction! You rub your chin and cheek and feel no sign of whiskers or stubble—you can't even tell when you're rubbing against the grain.

And there's no razor burn! Your face is totally comfortable as well as being totally smooth. All through the morning you surreptitiously feel your face, and you find yourself thinking of tomorrow's shave—which soap or cream to use, which aftershave...

You're hooked[9].

FIVE

Shaving step by step

IN the following chapters I explain in detail the process of shaving, following the chronological sequence of the shave. Each chapter focuses on a single part of the shave. Some steps are optional, and those I clearly indicate as such. The series of YouTube videos made by Mantic59[10] is an excellent complement to the information in this book.

Grain of your beard

Before you begin to shave, determine the grain of your beard: the direction of its growth. You must know this because your first pass is to shave *with* the grain, your second pass *across* the grain, and (later, after you're comfortable using the razor) a pass *against* the grain. You'll probably find that the grain has different directions on different parts of your face and neck. Part of learning to shave is learning the lineaments of your own face.

When you shave with a single blade (rather than a multiblade cartridge), you will make 2, 3, or even 4 passes—though when you begin, 2 passes are enough. The reason for the multiple passes is to get a close shave while using minimal pressure: instead of trying to achieve a close shave by pressing harder, you make more passes. Pressure produces nicks, cuts, and razor burn (scraping away the top layer of your skin). In shaving with a good safety razor, the weight of the razor is generally as much pressure as you want.

To determine the direction of your beard's grain, wait 12-24 hours after you've last shaved, then rub your fingertips (or the edge of a credit card or a cotton ball) over your beard. The rough direction is against the grain at that point.

For most men, the beard grows downward on the cheeks, so that part of the beard feels roughest if you're rubbing upward. But I discovered that at the corner of my right jaw, my beard grows horizontally toward my chin: at that point, against the grain is horizontally toward my ear. And just around the right side of my mouth, the grain tilts.

The grain on your neck probably has some odd directions. It's not unusual, for example, for the beard on the neck to grow upward, so that shaving downward is against the grain. One reason the neck is so often a shaving challenge is the irregularity of the grain of the beard there.

When you start, you may want to make a small sketch of your face and indicate the grain directions with arrows as a memory aid. Soon, though, you will know the grain of your beard by heart.

SIX

Prep

THE quality of your shave largely depends on how well you prepare your beard for the shave. A dry whisker, according to Gillette, is as tough as a copper wire of the same diameter—but a whisker, unlike copper, can soak up water and become soft. Good prep ensures that your whiskers soften. Inadequate prep leaves your whiskers tough, so the blade tugs, catches, and skips, giving you an uncomfortable and scraggly shave, complete with nicks and cuts, and a blade that's now dull.

Shaving resembles painting in that you spend a good amount of time preparing the surface before actually picking up brush (or razor). The actual painting/shaving occurs only toward the end of the process and goes more or less easily (and works more or less well) depending on the quality and thoroughness of your prep as well as on your skill and the quality of the tools.

Step 1: Shower

For most men, it's a good idea to shave after showering: the hot water and steam of the shower give a good start to wetting the beard. Some men, though, find that showering makes their skin sensitive and prone to irritation; those should shave *before* showering.

A moisturizing hair conditioner used on your beard in the shower can soften even a tough beard. Be sure to look for a hair conditioner that softens hair—conditioners come in different types[11].

Guys who shower in the evening might consider shaving then as well. For a novice, that's a particularly good idea: in the evening, you're not rushed, so you can take your time as you master the technique. And the ritual of wetshaving is relaxing, as noted above.

Step 2: Wash your beard

Even though I've just showered, I still wash my beard at the sink with soap and water and then rinse. Some guys find that they get a better shave if they don't use soap but just rinse their face with water. Because individuals differ so much, you have to experiment to find what works best for you. For me, it's washing my beard with soap and water.

I at first used Baxter of California's Vitamin E-D-A Cleansing Bar, a very good soap sold by QED. (See Appendix for a list of vendors, with links.) But then I found an even better pre-shave soap: Musgo Real Glyce Lime Oil Soap, specifically designed as a pre-shave soap and sold by Barclay Crocker, Lee's Razors, Sesto Senso, and others. Wash your beard with this soap, partially rinse with a splash of warm water, and then lather—and enjoy a fine shave.

Obviously, since you're running a sharp blade over your face, your face should *definitely* be clean. No grime, please.

Step 3: Apply a pre-shave [optional]

Before you lather, you may want to apply a pre-shave to your wet beard. Some pre-shaves are applied before the first pass, others before each pass. With any of the pre-shaves, try shaving a week with it, then a week without, to see whether it actually helps your shave. (Some find a pre-shave helpful, others do not.) Also experiment using a pre-shave before the first pass only, and before each pass. I generally use no pre-shave treatment and instead just rely on a good lather.

Pre-shave creams

Proraso, an Italian company, makes a cream[12] that can be used both as a pre-shave and an aftershave. You can find it at several of the vendors in the list. When I use this, I apply it only once, before lathering for the first pass, and leave it on for about five minutes before lathering. Some apply it before showering, and leave it on in the shower. As the name says, it can also be used as an aftershave.

Crema 3P and PREP Classic Cream are Italian pre-shave creams similar to Proraso. Another Italian pre-shave is a gel: Floïd Sandolor Preshave Gel. All are available from RazorandBrush.com

Trumper Coral Skin Food

Coral Skin Food is normally an aftershave: a soothing balm and skin treatment that's quite pleasant. Dr. Chris Moss, a long-time safety- and straight-razor shaver and author of *The Art of the Straight-Razor Shave*[13], discovered that it makes a very good every-pass pre-shave: apply it to the wet beard just before lathering for each pass.

100% glycerine

Dr. Moss, on inspecting the ingredients in Coral Skin Food, noticed that glycerine was included, so he decided to try 100% glycerine as an every-pass pre-shave. It turns out to have much the same effect as the Trumper Coral Skin Food—at a much lower price. You can find 100% glycerine[14] at health-food stores and some drugstores.

Taylor of Old Bond Street Pre-Shave Herbal Gel

TOBS, as Taylor's is often called, makes a pre-shave herbal gel that some men with tough beards have found effective. After the beard is washed and rinsed, you rub the gel into the wet beard and then let it sit for a minute or two. You could do this step before the shower, for example. Then lather on top of the gel and shave as you normally do.

Pre-shave oils

Some men use pre-shave oils. I've never liked oils as a pre-shave (though later I discuss their use in the final shaving pass), so I don't have much to say about them save that they exist. It's not clear to me that they're compatible with a good lather or good for your shaving brush.

If you want to try a pre-shave oil, try using a few drops of jojoba oil or olive oil, recommended by several shavers. Pacific Shaving Company's All-Natural Shaving Oil seems to include some emulsifier so that it doesn't feel as oily as other shaving oils. Later in the book I discuss a variety of pre-shave oils.

Step 4: Apply hot towel [optional]

If you get a shave in a good barber shop, the shave is preceded by moist, hot towels placed over the face. This further softens the beard. There's a good description on BadgerandBlade of a hot-towel technique[15]. Essentially, it consists of the following: Wash and lather your beard, and then wrap a moist hot towel around it, lean back, and meditate quietly for 1-3 minutes. The moist heat of the towel combined with the lather softens the beard remarkably. Then remove the towel, re-lather, and start the first pass.

If you have a microwave: put a damp towel in the microwave for 45 seconds. You can buy a pack of barber towels to use if you like this technique. If you're a true sybarite, spritz a little hydrosol[16] or other fragrance on the damp towel before heating it.

This step is *not* optional if you suffer from razor bumps.

Step 5: Apply lather

Lather is created from either shaving soap or shaving cream by using a shaving brush and hot water. It takes some practice to learn to create a good lather, so be patient and observe how it works. Let's look at it step by step.

- Shaving brush
- A good lather
- Shaving cream
- Shaving soap

Shaving brush

The best shaving brushes are made of bristles taken from the Asian badger and come in several grades[17]. (If you want to avoid animal products, you will be interested in brushes that use synthetic bristles.[18]) The brushes are made by hand[19] (you can even make your own[20]) and there are clear differences[21] between pure, best, and silvertip badger brushes, though the categories not well defined and vary by manufacturer.

Some users find that their new badger brush has a distinct badger odor. The odor goes away with use, and its departure can be hastened by shampooing the brush and using it with a shaving cream, such as Proraso, that has its own strong fragrance (menthol and eucalyptus, for Proraso).

Vulfix brushes[22] are popular. Probably the two most popular brushes from the line are the Vulfix 2235 and the 2234. The 2235's *loft* (bristle length) is longer (50mm vs 47mm for the 2234), so it's a bit more flexible. The 2235 has a larger *knot* (diameter at the base of the bristles)—23mm vs 22mm for the 2234—so it holds a bit more water/lather. The brushes are very close overall.

Simpson brushes[23] have been a step up from Vulfix, but recently Simpsons was purchased by Vulfix and the quality of the Simpsons line may have changed. My Simpsons Emperor 3 in Super Badger, from a few years ago, is better than my Vulfix. The Emperor's bristles seem to have just the right "give" and density, and I liked its size. Although I like the Emperor 3 (the largest), as I became more experienced and started lathering on my face, I got an Emperor 2 (pictured). Both are excellent—but I have no personal experience with the current Simpsons. Some have said they are quite good, though.

My current favorites are the Rooney brushes[24]. I first got the Style 3 Large Super Silvertip, but as I found a smaller brush more to my taste, I got both a Style 3 Small Super Silvertip and a Style 2 Super Silvertip. (Style 2 comes only in Small.) Those are now among my favorite brushes—though, obviously, this can change. You will note in the photo on the following page that Styles 2 and 3 have a slightly larger handle than Style 1, one reason I prefer them.

The Style 3 Small has a slightly shorter loft than the Style 2 (55mm vs 60mm), so is a slight bit stiffer. I ultimately got a Style 2 Finest and it is today my favorite brush—beautiful and functional. (If you ever do get a Finest, don't use it in highly pigmented shaving creams—for example, Geo. F. Trumper Rose, D.H. Harris Lavender— since that might stain the pure white bristle tips.)

Rooney has now come out with the Heritage line of high-quality brushes, but those brushes are for me too dense and stiff. Others, however, describe their Heritage brushes as the perfect brush. The Emilion seems to be particularly popular. Again: which brush is "excellent" varies by shaver.

If you can afford it, I *highly* recommend the Rooney Small Super Silvertip—in any of the three styles—as your first shaving brush. A less expensive alternative is noted below. This photo by Vintage Blades LLC shows, left to right, Styles 1, 2, and 3 in Small.

I did try a Rooney Style 3 Small Finest. Oddly, it didn't work at all for me—though it might for you. The bristles were so stiff and dense I could not work up a good lather—the same problem I had with the Heritage brush. On the other hand, as I said, the Style 2 Small Finest is currently my favorite brush. With resilient bristles and not so dense, it's easy to work up a good lather, and it holds enough lather for many passes.

I should point out that the guy who bought that Style 3 Finest brush from me likes it a lot—and the Heritage line is popular as well. So it depends on what you want in a brush.

Simpson brushes (measurements[25]), Rooney brushes, and Omega brushes[26] (measurements[27]) are all excellent. Both Rooney and Omega Silvertip brushes are amazingly soft and thick—quite a luxurious feel.

Savile Row brushes (from QED) are also nice—soft, not stiff. Shavemac brushes[28] are beautiful, but too stiff for my taste. G.B. Kent brushes[29] are *extremely* nice and do an excellent job building a lather from shaving soap. The pictured BK4, the best all-round size, is sold by The Gentlemen's Shop. One shaver commented that the BK4 can work up a good lather from a pot roast. ☺

Another line of high-end brushes are those made by Plisson, a French manufacturer who provides handles made of horn, ebony, briarwood, rosewood, and other natural sources, as well as handles of brass and acrylic. Some consider the Plisson High Mountain White the best of all brushes. I have one and still like the Rooney 2 Finest better.

Superior Brushes[30] are made to order by a couple of firefighters in Clovis NM: you specify the knot size and the color and style of the handle. The brushes come in four knot sizes: 20mm, 22mm, 25mm, and 30mm. I have one of each, and all are excellent. The brushes are very reasonably priced. The Superior 22mm or 25mm Silvertip makes an excellent first brush.

All the brushes mentioned above are high-end, some higher than others. If those are too pricey, look for something cheaper, but I would say that anything costing less than $20 is suspect. Probably the best starter brush for a modest price is the Edwin Jagger Best Badger from Crabtree & Evelyn[31] or The English Shaving Company[32]. The English Shaving Company offers a wide variety of best badger brushes; C&E offers one. The prices are almost the same, even with shipping. The best size for a beginner is the Medium.

With brush handles made of natural substances such as wood or horn, you have to be more aware of possible water damage, though some believe that wooden-handled brushes do just fine[33]—many boats are, after all, made of wood.

You may also be interested in the various innovations now appearing among shaving brushes[34]—variable-loft brushes, for example.

Lather is produced from a shaving cream or shaving soap (discussed below), so sometimes the question arises, "Which brushes are best for shaving cream, which best for soap?" In fact, any brush can do a fine job with both soaps and creams. You learn how to use the brush, and you learn how to create lather (see below), and that's it.

So don't worry about soap brushes vs. cream brushes—it's a red herring. Just pick a brush that *you* like. For me, that's a softer brush; for others, it's a stiffer brush. One video[35] shows a soft brush (claimed by some not to be a "soap brush") quickly working up an excellent lather from a hard soap.

I took the Simpson Major Super Badger Travel Brush on a trip, and I loved it—an exceptionally good brush on par with the Simpson's Emperor. (If you do a lot of travel, Em's Place has some nice accessories[36].) Although the Simpsons Major looks small, it holds plenty of lather for 4 passes—the brush is very like the Emperor 2.

My favorite brushes

Each shaver will have his own preferences with regard to every aspect of shaving: methods, equipment, and supplies. Still, I do get asked which brushes I prefer, so here are my own favorites.

The top tier are the Rooney Size 1 Super Silvertips (Styles 1, 2, and 3) and the G.B. Kent BK4 and an Omega Silvertip that I love for its softness. The Rooney Style 2 Finest is exceptional, of course, and expensive. The other five are much less expensive and do a great job.

Then I have a number of other favorites. There's the scrubby crowd: the Simpsons Duke 3 Best, Commodore 3 Best, and Chubby 1 Best. Less scrubby but very nice are the Simpsons Harvard 3 Best, Emperor 2 Super, Emperor 3 Super, and Persian Jar 2 Super. The Plisson brass-handled size 12 Chinese Grey has an interesting coarse feel and does a fine job, as does the Plisson size 12 White.

Those are the brushes for which I most often reach. All are great for face lathering, and all create a fine lather quickly.

Care of your brush

If you soak your brush prior to shaving, do *not* use boiling-hot water. Just hot from the tap is fine. Boiling-hot water will ruin the bristles. (I don't soak the brush—I simply hold it under the hot-water tap until it's full of water.)

When you complete your shave, rinse all the lather out of your brush with warm or hot water, and then do a final rinse of the clean brush using cold water. (The hot water should not be so hot you cannot keep your hands in the stream.) Reason: the hair shaft is covered with cuticle—overlapping scales somewhat like roofing shingles[37]. In hot water, these scales stand out from the hair shaft; in cold water, the scales hug the shaft tightly. This is one reason shaving with hot water is more comfortable than shaving with cold: hot water opens the cuticle and the whisker absorbs water more readily. And this is why beauticians do a final shampoo rinse with cool water: so the cuticle lies flat and the hair will look shiny instead of dull.

You may want a stand for the brush[38] (it grips the brush at the base of the bristles, bristles downward), but that's definitely optional. (Simpson states that their brushes should simply stand on the base of the handle to dry after you've rinsed the bristles, first in hot water then in cold, shaken the brush well, and dried it on a towel—no stand needed.) Indeed, if you collect brushes, you will have to improvise a large rack. I use a couple of 4-tier spice racks to hold my collection of brushes and razors.

Over time brushes may become slightly waterproof from hard-water deposits. Since the brushes are made of (badger) hair, they can be easily restored by washing them with a good shampoo and conditioner.

Emily from Em's Place has various reference articles at ShaveInfo.com, including some videos on a brush cleaning method[39] that produces excellent results. You first soak the brush for about 5 minutes in warm (not hot) water with some dishwashing detergent (not the kind you put in a dishwasher, but the kind used in hand-washing dishes), swirling it from time to time. (Another option: use Johnson Baby Shampoo: very gentle and neutral pH.) Then mix 9 parts water, 1 part white vinegar and a dash of 100% glycerine (available at a drugstore or healthfood store) and soak the brush in that for about 10 minutes. Rinse the brush, and you will find that it's now soft and water-absorbent.

As described in the later section on "Cleaning your razor," you can also use an ultrasonic cleaner to clean the brush—you immerse *only* the bristles, **not** the base of the knot.

M.A.C. brush cleaner[40] is intended for cleaning make-up brushes, but a shaver ventured to clean his shaving brush with it and found that it did an excellent job.

Cleaning the brush may not be needed if you have soft water and are careful about rinsing the brush after use. And it certainly isn't needed so often as cleaning your razor.

A good lather

Normally you can simply use hot water from the tap to make your lather, but if you live where the water is very hard, try using distilled or "purified" water, sold cheaply in drugstores for use in steam irons. You can heat it ahead of time on the stove or use something like the Sunbeam Hot Shot[41] to heat it in the bathroom. (The Hot Shot brings a pint of water to 180° in a minute.) Or you can use a hot-water dispenser like those made by Zojirushi[42]; these maintain water at a pre-set temperature (175°, 195°, or 208° F). Or the UtiliTEA[43] kettle will heat water to the temperature you set but no hotter.

The defining characteristic of a good lather is that it's dense and heavy with microscopic bubbles. Larger bubbles indicate either too much water or water added so fast that it could not be worked into the lather. Your whiskers are softened by absorbing water, and a thick, heavy lather holds water against the stubble in addition to lubricating the skin so the razor glides easily.

A good lather may be somewhat drier[44] and thicker than you expect—or it may be wetter. Experiment to find the best lather for you.

Use the brush to work the lather thoroughly into your beard. You need only enough lather to fully cover the whiskers—that is, the lather need not be deep on your face. Keep the lathered brush (whether using cream or soap) to re-lather your face prior to each shaving pass. Rinse your face after each pass before relathering: lather is always applied to a wet beard. Each pass with the razor requires a lathered (and thereby lubricated) face.

Lather can be built either in a lathering bowl or directly on your beard. I initially used a lathering bowl, but once I learned the look and feel of good lather, I switched to lathering directly on my beard.

Using a lathering bowl

When asked the best shaving tip they had read, quite a few shavers said that it was to use a lathering bowl. Building the lather in a bowl helps you observe the lather as you experiment, trying different proportions of water and shaving cream or soap until you learn to get a lather you like. You can rub the lather between thumb and finger to see how protective and slick it is.

Because a bowl is normally used as a container, the natural tendency is to think that the lathering bowl's purpose is to hold the lather, into which you dip the brush and then apply—much as a paint can holds the paint that the paintbrush applies.

Not so: the lather's in the brush, not in the bowl. The bowl merely presents a surface of a convenient shape for building a lather. This fact becomes obvious when you create the lather not in a bowl, but directly on your beard. I first did this on a trip, having opened my suitcase to find a broken lathering bowl. With no bowl, I found that the lathered brush held plenty of lather for multiple passes.

It's difficult to see how the lather's doing if the lathering bowl is white, so use a bowl that's a relatively dark color. Other than that, any roughly hemispherical bowl that's about 5″ across and 2.5″-3″ deep will work fine. Start with a cereal bowl from your kitchen.

The lathering bowl—important point—should have been filled with hot water to sit for a while (while you shower, for example). Few enjoy cold lather. Then empty the hot water from the bowl, rinse the brush in hot water, and proceed. Obviously, you can use hot water from the tap to heat the bowl, even if you're going to use distilled water from the hot-pot for the lather.

With a large brush, the bowl works better than building the lather directly on your beard. The Edwin Jagger Medium Best Badger is a reasonable size for face lathering, and you can work it smartly against your beard, but a really large brush doesn't get enough action merely against the beard. For large brushes, the bowl lets you work the lather into the brush better, and also allows you to adjust water amounts. But: the lather's in the brush, not the bowl.

Another important point: badger brushes hold a lot of water, and if you fail to work all that water into the lather at the outset, you'll find that in the second and third pass the lather has become thin and worthless. So, *especially* with a brush that's both large and stiff, you should "pump" the brush (and this is where a lathering bowl is helpful), combined with the usual swirling and stirring motions. You pump the brush by working it up and down; this ensures that the water at the base of the brush gets worked into the lather.

Don't pump it so vigorously that you break or damage the bristles—just enough to work the lather fully into the brush and the brush's charge of water fully into the lather. Experience will be your guide. Brushes that hold much water will therefore require a bit more shaving cream or shaving soap for a proper lather than a brush holding less water.

Some large-knot brushes, like the Omega Silvertips, are soft and flexible enough so that the pumping action usually happens automatically as you swirl and stir up the lather, so no special pumping is normally required.

The video referenced above[45] shows the pumping and the quick creation of lather. The brush is the Kent BK8, a softer brush that some presume is "not good for soap." The video clearly shows this notion is false. The soap is Kent shaving soap (same as Mitchell's Wool Fat shaving soap), and the lathering bowl is the Moss Scuttle (see below). And the water is soft. The BK8 can be used for face lathering, but the BK4 is a better size for that.

A video by Mantic[46] covers the full range of lathering options and is well worth viewing.

Em's Place has more information[47] on lathering from both soaps and creams. Razor-skipping when you shave (razor head not gliding smoothly across your skin, but seeming to "stick" and then skip) might be due to hard water, but it also might be a problem with the lather[48]. If you switch creams and soaps a lot (trying different samples, for example), you may not find the sweet spot for a particular cream or soap and be using too much (or too little) water.

Try making some practice lather, starting with a lather that's clearly dry and adding just a little water as you work the brush with the soap or cream. Work in the water each time and then feel the lather between thumb and forefinger. At first, it will be almost sticky. Then, as you hit the sweet spot, the appearance of the lather will change, and it will feel slick. As you continue adding water, you'll find that soon the lather is again sticky.

After several practice lathers using the same cream (or soap) each time, you'll know the look and the feel of a good lather. You can then transfer this knowledge to other creams or soaps, which may require a different amount of water for the sweet spot. After you know it, the sweet spot is clear—some say the lather "explodes" at that point—but it doesn't so much increase in volume as change state.

You'll note the continuing theme in shaving: the need to experiment and to find what works well for you. Guidance (as from this book) can be helpful, but the final test is your own experience.

Building lather on the beard

Although I began by building the lather in a bowl—quite useful for reasons explained above—I now build the lather directly on my beard. This gives a good lather and also ensures that the lather is thoroughly worked into my beard. The general technique is as follows.

Run lots of hot water over your brush, then shake it two or three times. Charge this more-than-slightly-damp-but-much-less-than-sopping-wet brush with a certain amount of soap or cream (you'll learn by experience) and rub it thoroughly all over your wet beard.

Then run a little hot water into the center of the brush and rub the brush briskly over the soap or cream that's on your beard. As you brush vigorously over all your beard, the lather will build.

You may have to add another driblet of hot water, but perhaps not. Continue to work the lather until you're satisfied with the quantity and the quality of the lather.

Take care not to add too much water along the way—experience will tell you the right amount, so long as you're paying attention to what you're doing and the outcomes that result. The brush itself will hold plenty of lather for the later passes.

The warming scuttle

The Moss Scuttle[49] (shown at right) allows you to enjoy warm shaving lather, a real treat. It consists of two bowls, the upper sitting in and attached to the lower (so it doesn't fall off when you empty the water).

To use: fill both bowls with water as hot as you can get it from the tap. Leave the hot water in the bowls while you shower.

Then empty out all the hot water, and fill only the inner (bottom) bowl with hot water: this will keep the upper bowl hot. Rinse the brush with hot water, then load it with soap or cream and build the lather. After the first lathering, let the brush sit in the hot upper bowl while you shave. Then, when you relather before the next pass, the brush and lather will still be warm.

The upper bowl is generally too small to use as a lathering bowl—you want the lathered brush to fit snugly in the bowl to keep warm. The Moss scuttle comes in two sizes—small and large (see photo)—and the small size is right for all but quite large brushes.

Dr. Moss provides this information:

My experience is that if you make the water in the scuttle too hot it will encourage the lather to break down. The other thing is whether you are getting the proportions right when you make the lather. Here's the way I use the scuttle:

Fill scuttle with hot water in both compartments.

Soak brush in the hot water in the inner bowl.

Do other stuff – for me this means wash face and strop razor, but for you might include reading New York Post, write angry letter to editor, kick cat, and so on.

Empty scuttle.

Refill outer part only with hot water.

Shake out brush.

Place exactly one British Standard Fingertipful of cream on brush.

Work brush into inner bowl of scuttle, adding a few drips of hot water as necessary.

Make lather on face, dipping brush tip in hot sink water judiciously if necessary (it usually is).

Place brush back in scuttle and push down to maximise brush to scuttle contact area.

Shave, or something like it.

Relather with hot lather. Place brush back in scuttle *q.v. step#10*

Shave again in some other direction.

Relather for the bits that need it. Place brush you know where.

Shave in another direction, removing tiniest traces of beard.

Rinse face, brush, and scuttle in desired order.

Kick cat.

Go to work, pretend to enjoy it.[50]

Georgetown Pottery[51] makes a scuttle that serves the same function as the Moss Scuttle, though with a slightly different design.

One shaver has pointed out that a *thick* ceramic bowl will hold quite a bit of heat once it's hot all the way through, and can keep the lather warm for the entire shave. Others put their lathering bowl in a sink filled with hot water. Some find a pair of bowls to use in the manner of the Moss Scuttle. I usually just stand my brush on its base between passes, and the lather stays warm enough for me.

Shaving cream

Shaving creams come in a wide variety, including unscented creams (for example, Truefitt & Hill Ultimate Comfort) for those with sensitive skin. (If your skin is sensitive, it's a good idea to test any new product—cream, soap, aftershave, etc.—on the inside of your forearm before using it on your face.)

Cyril R. Salter Mint is a great summertime shaving cream. J. M. Fraser's Shaving Cream[52] has a light lemony fragrance, creates a good lather, is highly effective at softening the beard, and gives a fine shave.

It's nice to have a few shaving creams for variety. Taylor of Old Bond Street Avocado has received high praise[53]:

> I couldn't agree more on the [Taylor's] avocado. The scent is nice and light but not as luxurious as some others. The real value for me is the lubricity you described [presumably from the avocado oil (persea gratissima) in the formulation] along with zero irritation. The absence of coloring and heavier scent additives I think is what drives this. In my opinion, this benefit makes this the ideal cream for a newbie, which I am.

Taylor of Old Bond Street is one of the "three T's" of fine English shaving creams and soaps. The other two are Truefitt & Hill and Geo. F. Trumper. All three make exceptional shaving creams.

For true luxury, it's hard to beat Castle Forbes shaving cream, available in lavender, lime, or cedarwood. It's pricey (perhaps better to receive as a gift than to buy), and it produces a wonderful, thick lather. Other luxury creams are those from D.R. Harris, Floris London, Acqua di Parma, Penhaligon, Institut Karité, and others. Particularly nice luxury creams are made by The Gentlemens Refinery.

Some artisanal soap makers also make shaving creams. Look for the shaving creams at Em's Place, Mama Bear, Razor and Brush, and Saint Charles Shave. Em's Place has lathering shaving cream that comes in a plastic dispenser bottle: you squirt some onto your brush and then build the lather—it produces a fine, thick, moisture-laden lather. The dispenser makes this an ideal shaving cream for those who shave in the shower, though I use it frequently and I shave at the sink.

You can buy shaving creams in a tube or a tub. Generally speaking, the price per ounce in a tube is twice what it is for the same cream in a tub. Some excellent shaving creams, though, are available only in a tube—Proraso shaving cream (from Italy) is one example, and it's not expensive. Other "tube only" shaving creams that are Musgo Real (from Portugal), Speick, and Tabac (both from Germany).

Using a lathering bowl

To produce lather with shaving cream using a lathering bowl, apply a small amount of shaving cream ("about the size of an almond" is the usual suggestion) to the wet brush and then work the brush in the empty, heated lathering bowl, using a motion that's more than stirring but less than whipping. (If you whip vigorously, you'll get a lot of lather, but it will be unprotective because it contains too much air. You want a stiff, dense lather that contains water more than air.) The stirring motion will create a thick, creamy lather. Too much water makes a lather that's bubbly and runny rather than dense.

Because shaving creams can produce quite a bit of (unprotective) lather even if you use too little shaving cream, you should experiment to make sure you're using enough. Perhaps initially you should try using a dollop the size of a large Brazil nut instead of an almond, then in later shaves cut back until you find the right proportion. The lather should be dense enough—and contain enough water—to do a proper job.

An illustrated guide[54] shows one method of lathering with a cream. In this guide, he uses water from a hot-pot—I use hot water from the tap, but my water is relatively soft. If your water is very hard, using distilled (or "purified") water from the drugstore is a good idea, as mentioned above.

I get the best results if I start creating the lather after shaking water from the brush, so that the brush isn't terribly wet, and then add driblets of hot water as I develop the lather. This produces an abundant and substantial lather that's suitably wet—but not too wet.

Also, since the brush is relatively dry (and not dripping water), I twirl the brush briefly over the cream in a tub to pick up a small amount of the cream, rather than dipping some out with my finger or a small spatula.

Lathering directly on your beard

To build lather from a shaving cream directly on your beard, without a lathering bowl: Twirl the wet (but shaken out) brush in the tub of cream to coat the tips with cream. Then work the brush on your wet beard to create a thin layer of almost pure shaving cream over all your beard. As you add water to the brush and continue to work it on your beard, the lather will build. If you're using cream from a tube instead of a tub, just squeeze a small amount (about the size of an almond) and rub it onto your cheeks or place it on the brush tips and then brush vigorously to work up the lather.

Shaving soap

Shaving soap is a nice (and cheaper) alternative to shaving cream. The "three T's" (Geo. F. Trumper, Taylor of Old Bond Street, and Truefitt & Hill), well known for their shaving creams, also make triple-milled shaving soaps, as does D.R. Harris, whose soap makes an exceptionally good lather. Another favorite from Britain is Mitchell's Wool Fat Shaving Soap[55]. Tabac[56] and Gold-Dachs Rivivage[57], both from Germany, are fine shaving soaps. Virgilio Valobra[58], an Italian company, makes quite a wonderful soft almond-scented shaving soap—it comes in a bar but is the consistency of clay so that you mash it it into a

mug or bowl. Institut Karité shaving soap (25% shea butter) and Durance L'òme[59] are exceptionally good shaving soaps from France.

Shaving soaps handmade by artisans are a particularly pleasant luxury—they make great soaps in a range of fragrances much broader than a traditional soap company can offer. Look in the Appendix for these vendors:

- Em's Place
- Honeybee Spa
- Mama Bear
- QED
- Saint Charles Shave
- Tryphon (Razor and Brush)

Their full range of products—beyond shaving soaps—is worth exploring. Their soaps include unscented varieties for those whose skin reacts to fragrances.

Honeybee Spa, QED, Mama Bear, and Tryphon make shaving soap in stick form—*shaving sticks.* These are pleasant to use and handy for travel. QED's Mocha-Java shaving stick is especially delectable. Valobra, Erasmic, Arko, Wilkinson, Boots, Palmolive, D.R. Harris, and Taylor of Old Bond Street also make excellent shaving sticks. (Some of those are simply cylinders of soap—some are foil-wrapped. For travel, they fit into a tall plastic prescription pill bottle.) The lather from all of these shaving sticks is excellent, but the D.R. Harris shaving stick is particularly good.

You can also make your own shaving sticks from any easily-melted shaving soap (not the triple-milled soaps). For example, take a Honeybee Spa shaving soap puck and, after melting it, pour it into a shaving stick container. It's a simple process[60], but be careful not to get the soap too hot, lest you lose or alter the fragrance.

Lather from shaving soap

In addition to my procedure described below, the instructions from Classic Shaving[61] are helpful, with this amendment: give the wet brush a shake or two so that it doesn't hold so much water, and it will pick up the soap better—you can add more water as you work up the lather. Also take a look at this excellent tutorial[62] (with photos).

Until I started learning again the practice of wetshaving, I hadn't realized that lather is **not** created in the shaving soap container. The brush's initial encounter with the soap—rubbing the soap with the tip of the damp brush until a lather starts to form—is simply to charge the brush with soap, with the soaped brush then used to build the lather in the (empty, hot) lathering bowl or directly on the wet beard. That's why some shaving soaps are sold in containers barely large enough to hold the soap—Truefitt & Hill, Geo. F. Trumper, and Taylor of Old Bond Street soaps, for example.

When you're charging the brush with soap, the brush should not be dripping water. As noted above, give it a good shake or two, and then rub it briskly over the surface of the soap—it will then pick up enough soap to create a good lather. Some prepare the surface of the soap by running a little hot water over the surface and letting it sit while they shower, but I simply use the wet brush on the dry soap.

Using a lathering bowl

If you're building the lather in a lathering bowl, you charge the brush with soap—rubbing the tips of the more-than-damp-but-not-really-*wet* brush briskly over the soap until a lather starts to form. Continue rubbing for 30-45 seconds more, then transfer the brush full of soap to the lathering bowl and work it as described above for shaving cream, adding driblets of hot water until you have a satisfactory lather. Be careful not to add too much water, or the lather will be too thin for the later passes. As with the shaving cream, try making several lathers for practice.

Lathering directly on your beard

With shaving soap, you have a choice: a shaving stick or soap in a container. The shaving stick, highly recommended for the newbie, is also nice when traveling. With the shaving stick, you always build the lather on your beard, though once it's started you *could* work it up in a bowl—but why bother? In either case, the brush itself will hold all the lather you need for the later passes.

For a shaving stick

The shaving stick is the easiest way to get a good lather from a shaving soap. Rub the stick against the grain all over your wet beard, including your upper lip. The stubble will scrape off the right amount of soap for a good lather—and, of course, the thickest and toughest part of your beard will scrape off the most soap: a plus. Brushing your beard vigorously with the wet brush will start to build the lather. Add a little hot water to the center of your brush and continue to work the brush on your beard until all the soap that was applied has been worked into the lather and you have the lather you want. Again, experiment to find the amount of water that works best.

For soap in a mug

Rub your wet (but shaken out) brush briskly around over the top of the shaving soap, rubbing soap into the brush. When a lather starts to form, continue rubbing until the brush picks up enough soap—as much as a shaving stick would put on your beard. Brush vigorously over your wet beard and the lather will start to build, though at this point your beard will have more soap than lather.

Add a driblet of hot water to the brush's center and continue to brush vigorously, working up the lather. You may have to add a little more water to produce a sufficiently wet and dense lather, but working the lather around on your beard is all to the good. There's no rush: enjoy the process while your whiskers soak up water and soften. Experiment over several shaves with more water and with less to find the sweet spot for the lather.

Superlather

A "superlather" uses both shaving soap and shaving cream—best seen in a video[63]. Use a lathering bowl and begin to build the lather from a shaving soap—but also add a dab of shaving cream and work that into the lather as well. The result is a particularly slick and dense lather.

Another way to generate superlather: use a shave stick to apply soap to your prepped and wet beard, then twirl the brush in shaving cream and lather on your beard. The soap, together with the shaving cream, produces a thick, luxurious lather. I like QED's Lavender shaving stick and Em's Place Lavender shaving cream. A Fresh Lemon shave stick from Honeybee Spa works extremely well with the J.M. Fraser shaving cream. A shaver who doesn't particularly like either the l'Occitane Cade shaving soap or shaving cream alone found that the two work spectacularly together in a superlather.

SEVEN

The blade

THE blade and razor are the key components of the shave. Novices tend to focus more on the razor because it's more obviously interesting than the blade and also much more expensive. Yet the comfort and smoothness of your shave, once your prep and technique are good, will be about 70% from the blade and 30% from the razor.

High-quality double-edged blades generally run 35¢-55¢ each in a pack of 5 or 10—the "Swedish" Gillettes are 90¢ apiece—and as low as 9¢-14¢ each if you look around for lots of 100—for example, on eBay or from Razor and Brush. You can buy blades made in Germany, Turkey, Pakistan, India, Japan, Sweden, Egypt, Israel, the UK, the US, Russia, Poland, or other countries. Currently the best source, for range of brands and price, is RazorandBrush.com.

With the right cutting technique on a well-lathered face and softened beard, the typical blade can last about a week. Your experience may vary, depending on your prep, your beard, your skin, your technique, your razor, the brand of blade, the phase of the moon, etc. A range of 3-6 days is typical. There's no sense is trying to stretch a blade beyond a week—some blades will die gracefully, simply starting to pull and tug as they become dull, but others go out with a bang, and start nicking. Change the blade before that happens.

Double-edged blades thus cost substantially less than today's disposable multiblade plastic cartridges, which run as high as $3.50 each, and the usual rationalization for buying lots of delicious shaving equipment is that you'll be money ahead (eventually—sometime around the turn of the century) because of what you'll save on the blades. Remember: the blades are where Gillette makes its money—over time, the total spent on blades is much more than the price of the razor—so with less expensive blades you save money and over time save a lot.

Finding the right blade

Blades offer a couple of surprises. First, novices are surprised by how greatly blades differ in sharpness and smoothness. One shaver wrote[64]:

> Just started wetshaving 2 weeks ago...have only used Merkur blades since they came with the razor.
>
> Leisureguy suggested I order a 5-blade sampler with plan to try the blades in this order:
>
> – Merkur (already had) -> Israeli -> Derby -> Gillette -> Feather
>
> I rec'd my sampler yesterday and tried the Israeli this morning...WOW!!
>
> I could not believe the difference. My best shave so far by leaps and bounds. The razor was gliding across my face and by the 3rd pass it was the closest most comfortable shave I have had yet.

The second—and greater—surprise is that a given blade will get different responses from different shavers. For example, for me (and others) the Treet Blue Special blades (carbon steel) are sharp and smooth and produce a highly satisfying shave. Yet for some shavers they seem dull and tuggy.

Since a blade that someone else likes may not work for you—and a blade that they hate might work fine for you—trying blades yourself is the *only* way to find your own "best blade(s)." View skeptically comments like "this blade is excellent" or "this blade is terrible." Those reflect the speaker's experience. You *must* use the blades yourself to actually know how the blade will work *for you*.

The unpredictability of a shaver's response to any given brand of blade is mysterious but readily observed: Each brand has some who love it and some who hate it, and some who are indifferent. Some brands have a preponderance one way or the other, but even if only a few hate (or love) a brand, what if you are one of those few? You can't use the brand statistically: "I love this particular blade 60%, and hate it 35%, and am indifferent 5%." With an individual shaver and a particular blade, the judgment is 100%, whether love, hate, or indifferent. So each individual shaver has to try multiple brands to find the brand(s) that work best for him, rather than simply pick those that are (statistically) popular.

If it were not like this—if all shavers responded in the same way to a blade (which many novices believe is the case, and simply ask "Which blade is sharpest?" as if that would be the best blade for them)—then there would exist only one brand of blade: THE blade. Perhaps it would be sold in different colors of packages, or with different decorations printed on the blade, but everyone would use it because it is the universal "best" blade.

But life is not like that, and so blade sampler packs were developed to allow a shaver to try a wide variety of brands through one purchase. Originally, there was only one sampler pack, offered by LetterK on BadgerandBlade.com and ShaveMyFace.com. LetterK later established a Web site to sell a variety of sampler packs (WestCoastShaving.com), and two other vendors began selling sampler packs (ConnaughtShaving.com (UK) and RazorandBrush.com (US)). (Links for blade samplers are in the Appendix.)

I suggest getting the largest sampler pack, along with as many brands as you can buy locally. Initially, you won't be trying them all—they're for later. At first, try just one brand. (Guys for whom the Derby works will suggest you use a Derby; guys for whom the Israeli Personna works will suggest that, and so on. Just pick a brand.)

If that brand seems to work reasonably well, stick with it. If you are having trouble (with nicks or irritation), even though you're being careful with your prep, blade angle, and razor pressure, try a different brand. But as soon as you find a brand that seems to work, *stick with that brand* and don't try another brand until you're consistently getting good shaves—smooth, nick-free, and predictable. This may take from one to three months, and in some cases more.

This is important: if you keep changing blades as you learn, you will find it difficult to develop your groove. It would be foolish if you used a different make of tennis racquet each set while you were trying to learn tennis. It would similarly be foolish to skip from brand to brand to brand of razor blade, one shave each: you would never then learn the particularities of a brand of blade and whether it actually works for you.

Therefore experienced shavers all recommend that, once you find a brand that seems to work reasonably well, be faithful to that brand until your technique is solid and you are good at the basic double-edged safety-razor shave. At that point, your prep is solid: you can easily create an excellent lather, and when you bring blade to beard, your beard is fully wetted and as soft as it's going to get. Moreover, when you shave, you're not hesitant: your strokes are smooth and efficient, and you seldom encounter a nick or any skin irritation. You enjoy your shave, and the result is a smooth face and a jolly outlook.

At this point, you're certainly ready to take your shave to the next level. If you followed the suggestion above, you already have the sampler pack with the greatest number of brands. If not, get it now. Then start working your way through the pack.

Why explore?

Of course, once you're getting good shaves, you might think, "Why try another brand? This one's doing okay. Better just to stick with it." Indeed some (probably most) shavers simply stick with the first brand they encounter that gives them a passable shave. I've read comments, "This brand tugs a lot, but when I'm finished, I have a good shave, so it's a good blade." In my view, if you find that a blade tugs a lot, it's not a good blade for you. Shaving is about the process as well as the end result: both should be pleasurable.

By continuing to explore even after you're getting good shaves with a particular brand, you might find a blade that takes your shave to a whole new level. That's most likely to happen if (a) you've so far been shaving with a limited range of blades—the usual suspects are Merkur, Israeli, Derby, Swedish Gillette, and Feather—and, (b) the best brand for you is not one of the common brands.

It may happen, of course, that your best brand may be the brand you're already using—though, if you haven't tried many different brands, it's unlikely: the range of blades is quite large, you'll discover. And it may be that none of the new brands you try will really astonish you with the excellence of the shave. But I think it's likely that you'll find a blade better than you imagined possible. You have much to gain and little to lose with the exploration.

My experience started with trying the usual beginner blades. The Merkurs were horrid for me (though they are very good for some), the Israelis and Derbys were okay, but they tugged too much where my beard was tough. The Swedish Gillettes are good but too expensive. The Feathers were sharp but I kept getting an occasional unpredictable nick—indeed, some experienced shavers can't use Feathers at all.

But when I started trying a wider variety of blades, I found a brand of blades that did indeed make me say, "Wow!" It cut smoothly, easily, and never produced a nick or any sign of irritation. It was the Treet Blue Special, and (of course) it does not work well for everyone. But I was one of the lucky ones. What a fine shave it gave!

I naturally recommended it to others, and some had the same reaction as I: shaving nirvana! Others, however, probably thought I was crazy, though I explained as clearly as I could that individual shavers have very different responses to any given brand, that this brand might not work for them, etc. And I thought that it was worth a try.

Don't try just that one brand, though: it probably won't be a transcendent blade for you—though it might. To maximize your chances of hitting the lucky strike, try as many brands as you can. If you're lucky, you'll find a blade whose excellence is beyond that of any blade you've tried before. At the very least, you will do some inexpensive exploration and learning. Blade acquisition disorder is the least costly of all the shaving-related acquisition disorder, much cheaper than the acquisition disorders for razors, shaving creams, brushes, shaving soaps, aftershaves, and the like.

How to explore

To begin your blade exploration, load a new brand in a familiar razor and shave, maintaining the good technique that you've mastered. If you get a terrible shave, discard that blade and try another blade of the same brand—it may have just been a bad blade. (Rare, but it does happen.) If the second blade of the brand also gives you a terrible shave, discard it and mark that brand off the list: it's obviously not for you. EXCEPTIONS: If you have more than one razor, try the blade in another razor before you give up on it. A blade that's terrible in the HD might be wonderful in a Gillette Super Speed and vice versa. Also, some blades seem dull for the first shave or two, until the coating that covers the edge is worn away. Examples of this sort of blade: Sputnik, Astra Keramik, Dorco 301, Tiger, and Crystal.

Here's a careful and methodical approach. Call the blade that so far works best for you the "best blade."

1. Shave for a week with the current "best blade." This sets the baseline for comparison.
2. Shave for a week with a new brand of blade (unless it fails the test of two terrible shaves).
3. If the new brand is the better of the two, it is now your new "best blade": go to 2 to try another new brand.
4. If the new brand is not the better, go to 1.

By using this approach you're always comparing just two brands: your best so far and a new brand. That makes the comparison easy, and by always starting the comparison with a week shaving with the "best," you not only get a break from testing, you get a fresh reminder of what a blade that's good for you feels like before you try the next new brand.

Sometimes two different brands are almost equal in quality. To compare those, use each brand on alternate days so you can get a closer comparison.

On the other hand, you might want to move faster. Since at this point you're an experienced shaver with good technique, you will probably know after three or four shaves whether you like a new brand of blade or not. This greatly cuts down exploration time—but still it's a good idea to return periodically to your current "best blade" and shave a while with that to re-establish the standard. And remember that some brands will not shave smoothly for the first shave or two—your own response to a blade should be your guide, but try for three shaves at least before you decide a blade is dull.

As you explore, you'll find blades fall into one of three classes:

1. **Some won't work for you.** For such a brand, write a note on why it's not good for you (too dull, nicks too frequently,

irritates your skin—whatever), put the note and the remaining blades of that brand in an envelope, write the brand name on the envelope, and put it aside. After six months or a year, you might want to try the brand again to see whether things (your prep, technique, razor, etc.) have changed and the brand is now good for you. If it's still not your cup of tea, pass the blades along to someone else—for him, they could be a "best blade".

2. **Some will work fine**—just as good as the blade you've been using, or perhaps even a little better. You can add these to your rotation for variety.

3. And, if you're lucky, **one or two will make you say, "Wow!"** These blades are, for you, are truly exceptional: they shave so smoothly, so easily, so readily that you feel as though you've not really had a great shave before.

For me, my own current best blades are: Treet Blue Special, Astra Superior Platinum, Astra Keramik Platinum, the Wilkinson family (Economie, UK, and German), Zorrik, Polsilver Stainless, Iridium Super, Gillette Silver Blue, Elios, and Lord Platinum. "Swedish" Gillettes are quite good, but too expensive for me.

Once Feather and Tiger were among my favorites, but I finally decided that they were too ready to nick for no reason. They're like a high-powered but unstable motorcycle: great performance but unpredictable. You may have a different experience.

Gillette 7 O'Clock ExtraSharp blades (not to be confused with the 7AM brand) were so sharp that I couldn't comfortably use them—not erratic, just very, very sharp. Some guys like them a lot—but be careful with them. I will, of course, try them again someday.

With a microscope you can see the actual differences in the edges of different brands[65]. Microphotographs of the edges of Dorco New Platinum ST300,Personna Platinum Chrome ("Red Box"), Crystal Super + Platinum ("Israeli Personna"), and the Treet Blue Special show clear differences. The Treet clearly has a well sharpened edge—but still it doesn't work for some shavers, though it works extremely well for others. A series of reviews on ShaveMyFace of different brands of blades has a microphotograph of the blade being reviewed. The reviews are interesting, though of course the quality of the blade, in terms of the shave, is the reviewer's experience with the blade and not necessarily the experience that you or I would have. Different shavers have different responses to the same brand of blade.

Carbon-steel blades

Some blades (Treet Blue Special, Treet DuraSharp HiTech Steel, Treet Classic) are made of carbon steel rather than stainless steel. I know from using knives (and reading about straight razors) that carbon steel can take a sharper edge than stainless steel, but carbon steel does tend to rust. So if you find you like a carbon-steel blade, you have three choices:

a. Use a new blade for each shave (they're cheap).

b. Dry the blade after each use (*not* by rubbing it with a cloth but, for example, by shaking it well or using a hair dryer).

c. Easiest: After shaving, rinse the razor in hot water, give it a good shake, rinse the head in 91% or 99% rubbing alcohol, and then put it in a rack to dry. The alcohol displaces the water and then evaporates, leaving the blade dry so that it doesn't rust.

I go with option c., using an inexpensive 99% rubbing alcohol I bought at the local Safeway supermarket. (A 91% rubbing alcohol also works well and may be easier to find.)

I keep the rubbing alcohol in a one-cup canning jar, whose lift-off lid makes a tight seal that keeps the alcohol from evaporating. (I don't use the sealing ring at all.) Lift lid, swish razor head in the alcohol, replace lid, place razor on the rack to dry: quick and easy and the blade never rusts.

More about blades

Blades are generally printed with the manufacturer's name and other information, so the two sides—top and bottom—look different. You can put the blade in the razor with either side on top: it makes no difference. Since you use both edges of the razor as you shave—when one side of the razor has collected enough lather, you switch over to the other side for a while before you rinse the razor—the blade's two edges thus are worn down simultaneously.

Some novices wonder whether turning the blade over after a few shaves will make it last longer. It might, but given the price of blades, it doesn't seem to be worth the effort. Moreover, it's good to avoid handling the blade any more than necessary.

Some, as previously noted, find that a given brand of blade works well for them in one razor, but not in another. For example, a very sharp blade might work well for them in a Super Speed, but not in the HD. The practice of shaving: a continuing experiment.

One shaver who found Feather blades harsh tried pulling each edge of a new blade through a wine cork a few times before putting it into the razor. For him, this tamed the blade while leaving it still quite sharp. The technique has also been used on, e.g., American Personnas.

My own view of corking is that it's better to find a blade that works for you without corking. Moreover, a blade's edge is easily damaged, and the result of corking can be a blade that's much the worse for it—and for you. So my own inclination is to try more brands of blades before I try corking. Others like to do the corking. You decide for yourself which you want to do.

I do want to provide one blade warning. I had a chrome Merkur Slant Bar that provided me with lovely, perfect shaves when I used it with a Feather blade—and never a nick. So I decided I had to have a Slant Bar in gold. I got the gold Slant Bar, put in a new Feather—and Nick City! I was aghast. I tried again the next day: Nick City once more. The guy to whom I had sold my chrome Slant Bar happened to email me that he had received it, and I poured out my tale of woe. An incredibly nice guy, he offered to return the razor to me, and we worked out all the details.

When the chrome Slant Bar came back, I put in a new Feather blade and got a perfect, lovely shave, and not a nick. So I decided to try the gold Slant Bar one more time, and to make the experience exactly comparable, I loaded it, too, with a new Feather and shaved. Again, perfect, lovely shave, and not a nick. Exactly the same as the chrome Slant Bar—as one would expect, since the two are identical except for the plating.

So: it was a bad blade. I had read of this, but that was my first experience. I probably would have just tried another blade if (a) it wasn't my first shave with the new razor (thus blaming the razor instead of the blade, still thinking that all blades of a given make were the same); (b) I had previously encountered an instance of a bad blade (it's rare); and (c) I hadn't panicked, thinking I had just sold the one Slant Bar in all the world that would work for me.

Lesson learned: if you have a bad shave with a new razor, try a new blade. And if you then have a bad shave with the new blade, try a different brand of blade. Don't jump to the conclusion, as I did, that the razor is the problem.

Blade disposal

Because razor blades remain quite sharp even when too dull for shaving, disposal requires some care. (When I was growing up, all medicine cabinets had slots in the rear for disposal of razor blades. You don't see those anymore.) Plastic blade dispensers usually have a "used-blade" compartment on the bottom for safe disposal.

If you buy blades in bulk or buy a brand that lacks the dispenser, use a special receptacle for used blades rather than simply throwing the blades into the trash—razor blades can all too readily cut through plastic trash bags and into the hands lifting the bag. Proper disposal is especially important if the household includes small children or monkeys, but is important in any case—and, really, disposal of sharps is *always* worth doing with care.

You can easily find commercially made disposal safes for razors. The 99-cent Feather Blade Safe[66] works well, for example. But it's also very easy to make quite a good blade safe, as follows.

Take a small can containing a liquid—for example, a small can of evaporated milk or tomato juice—and drain the contents by punching two small holes in the top. Wash out the can, using the two holes. Then turn the can over and, using a hacksaw or a thin Dremel blade, cut a slit in the side, just under what was the bottom and is now the top. Make the slit just wide enough to admit a double-edged blade.

The can then sits (upside down, with the two small holes you made in the top now at the bottom) and you discard the blades through the slit, just under the now-top. When the can is full, a tap of a hammer permanently shuts the slit. There you have it: an opaque, unbreakable, metal blade safe with no lid to open.

EIGHT

The razor

THE focus of this book is the safety razor (like, for example, these at Classic Shaving[67]). Before the safety razor, there was the straight razor, but once the safety razor arrived, it quickly displaced the straight[68].

The blade is the very center of the safety razor system, and it was the blade that gave King Camp Gillette his opportunity and the challenge: to manufacture a sharp, disposable blade from thin, stamped steel. The safety razor holds the blade and presents the edge with a specific exposure and angle. The safety razor can be:

three-piece (like the early Gillette razors and the Merkur 1904, Classic, and Long Classic: top, platform, and handle);

two-piece (like the Merkur Futur, Hefty Classic ("HD"), Progress, and Slant Bar: top and platform-handle); or

one-piece (like the Vision, Gillette Super Speed, and other twist-to-open (TTO) razors: twisting the knob at the bottom in one direction opens butterfly doors for changing blades and, in the other, closes them to grip the blade for shaving).

Em's Place has a clear explanation (with photos) that explains these three types of razors[69].

In razors using double-edged blades, the blade is held between a top and a platform, with only the edge exposed. As the razor is tightened to grip the blade, the blade bends over the slight hump of the platform, making the edge rigid and presenting the edge at a specific angle, which differs slightly for different razors. (Single-edged blades, like those used in Gem razors and Schick Injectors, are rigid to start with because they are made of thicker steel, and thus do not have to be bent in the razor's grip as do the thin, double-edged blades.)

One error novices sometimes make is failing to tighten the razor sufficiently after inserting the (double-edged) blade. The top must be seated *firmly* onto the blade, to bend it over the platform and hold it securely. (The Futur's design cleverly finesses this error: the top *snaps* on, so if it's properly in place, it's holding firmly.)

The question is sometimes raised: *how* tight should the top be? So, a little scenario. You're going on a picnic. Just before you pack the jar of pickles, you open it and eat one. Then you put the lid back on and put the jar on its side in the basket. *That* tight: tight enough so the jar won't leak and the lid will stay on, but not so tight that your wife or girlfriend can't remove the lid at the picnic. (Although I do like the advice from one forum member: "Finger tight 'til she smokes, then back 'er off a quarter.")

A razor stand is helpful. You can buy a stand for a single razor from various places, but I enjoy a rack[70] that holds up to 12 razors: the razors in current use. A razor stand or rack is useful because you want the razor out where it can dry after you shave. Do not put it into a drawer—it won't dry so well and the blade's edge is more likely to be damaged in a drawer (much as you do not put your quality kitchen knives in a drawer, but keep them in a knife rack). Turnabout's fair play: a blade you nick will nick you.

Merkur razors

Of razors still in production, the Merkur line, made in Germany, are pre-eminent. Though occasionally a problem may be encountered (typically, uneven exposure, with the razor exposing one edge of the blade more than the other), your dealer will replace the problematic razor with a new one. Starting with a Merkur razor is the typical beginning for safety-razor shaving.

A post on BadgerandBlade has a good review[71] (with photos) of several Merkur safety razors. Some of the Merkur razors are available in either chrome- or gold-plated versions. There's no difference in performance, only in appearance. The Futur is available in a matte finish or a shiny finish in chrome or gold. Shavers who have the shiny version report that it is not difficult to hold—that is, it's not slippery.

Non-adjustable

Non-adjustable razors have a fixed blade angle and exposure. With no adjustment to consider (and tinker with), the novice shaver has one less thing to worry about—for example, if the shave is bad, the novice doesn't have to figure out whether it's his technique that's at fault or the particular setting of the adjustable razor (or both). Thus the recommended "starter razor" is non-adjustable.

Classic

The Classic line of Merkur razors all have the same head geometry—only the handles differ. Thus they all shave the same, though the different handles do indeed give them a different feel. Any of the Classic line would work well as the first razor for a beginning shaver. The same Classic head, more highly polished and with better chrome or gold plating, is also used in the Edwin Jagger line of safety razors, described below.

Hefty Classic (the "HD")

When experienced shavers were polled to find the razor that they would recommend for the novice, the HD was by far the preferred "starter razor." Having solid construction, thick handle, and good blade exposure and angle, it's a very good razor to learn on. It's more aggressive than the Gillette Super Speed (see below), but well within the capability of the novice shaver—though, as with all the razors, the use of a blade sampler pack is absolutely essential so that you can learn which brand(s) of blade you find best for you.

Some novices do find that the HD is too aggressive for them. They prefer a vintage Gillette Tech or Gillette Super Speed or a new Weishi razor, all milder than the HD.

If you go the vintage route, it's safer to buy via the Selling/Trading threads on the shaving forums than through eBay.

Classic

The same as the HD, but with a slimmer handle. Again, a good starter razor, lighter than the HD.

One benefit of the three-piece design is that the razor is completely flat when disassembled, making it easy to pack for travel.

Long-Handle Classic

This razor with the same weight of handle as the Classic, but longer. If you like a long-handle razor, this would be a good choice. I found that, for myself, the long handle was unhelpful and even seemed to get in the way. OTOH, this is very nice razor for women who shave their legs with a safety razor.

1904

This Classic is an underappreciated gem of a razor, whose handle has a somewhat ornate design from—guess!—1904. It was my second razor, and I continue to like it a lot. The little knob at the end of the handle is perfect when shaving against the grain. In fact, the only  drawback I've discovered is that it doesn't seem to come in gold.

38C

The Merkur 38C is new. It has the Classic head, but a longer, heavier handle with a spiral engraving. Unfortunately, due to its weight, I found the razor difficult to hold with wet hands—it tended to twist because of the spiral track. A chequered engraving would have been better for me. Some shavers don't have that problem—they rest the end of the handle on the little finger—and they love the razor.

Edwin Jagger razors

Edwin Jagger razors use the Merkur Classic head, but has Merkur do extra polishing. The heads are then plated (chrome or gold) to EJ specifications and attached to Edwin Jagger handles, available in three styles: Chatsworth, Loxley, and Georgian. The razors are elegant and those who prefer a larger handle should definitely consider them[72].

Slant Bar

The Slant Bar is an amazing razor and provides effortless, smooth shaves when used with a sharp blade that works for you. On the other hand, in the poll that named the HD as the preferred razor for a beginning shaver, *no one* recommended that a novice start with the Slant Bar. But when one has established good technique, the Slant Bar seems tailor-made for the combination of thick, wiry beard and sensitive skin. In my opinion, it should be your second razor.

The Slant Bar works best with a sharp blade. I recommend you try the Slant Bar only after you're getting consistently good shaves with your current safety razor—that is, your technique (maintaining the correct pressure and angle) is solid. Once your technique is polished, you can move to a new level of ease and closeness by using a Slant Bar.

The Slant Bar is handled *exactly* as a regular safety razor. The difference in performance is due not to any manipulation on your part but to the slant of the blade. Rather than chopping directly through each whisker, the slanted blade *slices* through the whisker when you pull the razor normally. This photo from Em's Place shows the slant clearly.

As you probably know, when you are, say, chopping carrots, you don't press the knife directly down through the carrot to the chopping block. Instead, you press it down while simultaneously pushing or pulling it slightly: slicing the carrot more than chopping it. Both methods work, but slicing requires much less effort.

The Slant Bar's way of holding the blade automatically slices (rather than chops) each whisker. Again: you don't wield it any differently than you would, say, the Merkur Hefty Classic. Shave with light touch and proper angle and don't even think about the fact that it's a Slant Bar (or Hefty Classic). The way the razor is constructed will take care of the cutting. Again: *light* pressure with the Slant Bar.

The 38C is also available with a Slant Bar head.

Open-comb vs. safety bar

Razors in the Merkur Classic series are available as "open-comb"—separated teeth instead of a safety bar. Open-comb razors have the blade either resting on the teeth (the Merkur and old Gillettes) or just above the teeth (the improvement introduced with the Gillette NEW IMPROVED (1921) and used in later models). The safety bar is a solid bar that rides on your skin just ahead of the blade as you shave.

The open comb was the original design, with the safety bar introduced later (easier to manufacture and not so fragile—drop an open-comb and you're likely to bend one of the teeth). The safety bar pushes away all the lather before the blade does its work, whereas the open comb leaves some lather as protection.

The photo on the left shows an example of an open-comb razor with the blade resting directly on the comb. This particular razor is the Merkur Hefty Classic Open Comb. On the right is the better design (in my opinion) with the blade held above the teeth by the "coat-hanger" profile of the base plate. The razor in that photo is the Gillette NEW, first offered in 1930 and one of my favorite razors.

An open-comb razor has a different feel from a safety-bar, and you can get a good shave with either. Most men opt for the safety bar. The quality of the shave is due mostly to the prep, the blade, and your technique, in any case.

Adjustable

Adjustable razors allow the shaver to adjust the angle and/or amount of blade exposed as you shave. It's not generally recommended to get an adjustable as your first safety razor for reasons stated above. Still, some novices do start with an adjustable and succeed.

The key to success with an adjustable razor is to start with the lowest (least aggressive) setting—the setting that has the least blade exposure and the flattest razor angle. Then advance the setting from shave to shave as needed to get a good shave. What you want is the *lowest* setting that produces a good shave, *not* the highest setting you can stand. The settings usually start with "1" as the lowest setting, with higher numbers denoting more aggressive settings.

Despite this advice, a surprising number of new shavers, through some sort of misplaced pride and machismo, will set the razor at its highest setting and get an amazing razor burn along with a harvest of bloody cuts. Don't make that mistake.

Progress

The Progress adjustable is a two-piece razor, unusual in that the cap has only one correct orientation. A line stamped on one end of the cap must be placed above the triangle stamped on one end of the base. It's a delight to use, though the correct angle for this razor differs quite a bit from the HD angle. But whenever you pick up a new razor you have to learn the proper angle for it—this is called "getting used to it" and is the same process as, for example, getting the feel for the right way to hold and cut with a new kitchen knife.

The Progress is well designed—a hefty, chunky razor that feels good in the hand. It's a favorite of many shavers, though some complain of uneven blade exposure. One shaver noted a cure[73]: press down on the top (with your fingers hooked under the base, like a syringe) and then tighten the knob. This prevents blade slippage as the tightening occurs.

Futur

The Futur is a good safety razor, heavy and substantial in a Teutonic way. The Futur is particularly aggressive, so by all means start at the setting 1, and gradually work your way up until you get a satisfyingly close shave. For me, that was at 1.5. Some guys have started with the setting at 4 or even higher and then regretted it bitterly. I found that I got the smoothest shave with the Futur if I rested the top on the skin being shaved, rather than the guard. Try different angles with it to find the angle that works best for you.

Some have found the Futur's adjustment to be stiff. One shaver offers this advice[74]: "First remove the blade, then set the head to position 6. Now press the blade carriage and the bottom of the head together, hold against the spring pressure, and unscrew the handle with your other hand. Now that you have it completely stripped down, put some silicone grease on the threads and reassemble in the reverse order of the above. This still leaves the adjustment heavy due to the spring pressure but makes the action a great deal smoother."

The clip-on top is, I think, a clever design: if you've snapped the top in place, the blade is properly gripped. No need to wonder about how firmly you should screw shut the top. Others don't like it so much. If you are changing blades, it's highly advisable to do so with dry hands and a dry razor. A slip can produce a cut.

Vision

The Vision (technically the "Vision 2000") is even more massive than the Futur but, in my experience, is easier to manipulate and provides a better shave. Some don't agree, of course—judgments of this sort are highly shaver-dependent.

I should note that some people have had problems with the Vision, though many have not. If you encounter a problem, it's handy to have what amounts to a Vision user's manual[75].

The Vision is heavy and, using a good blade that suits you, you can clearly hear it cutting the stubble, a sound like the distant rampaging of an elephant crashing through brush. I greatly enjoy using the Vision, and I rate it highly. It does require a certain amount of practice. I think it could even be a beginner's razor; others disagree.

Vintage razors

Vintage razors are easy to find: local flea markets and antique stores, elderly relatives, garage sales, eBay, and the Selling/Trading forums (at

BadgerandBlade, ShaveMyFace, or TheShaveDen) and the Sales Board of RazorandBrush are all good sources. There's great satisfaction in shaving with a vintage razor, and many deliver an excellent shave.

Gillette safety razors abound on eBay. BadgerandBlade has a good post with photos showing some common Gillette razors[76] you might encounter, and a reference site gives detailed information on how the production dates of Gillette razors[77] are coded.

Sometimes you will find that a vintage razor is damaged or bent, so inspect carefully any that you buy before using them.

As with most things in shaving, preferences in razors vary by shave: what works well for one person will not suit another.

Occasionally, a used razor will arrive with a blade in place. *Do not use that blade*—you don't know where it's been. Start with a new blade, fresh out of the package. Also, vintage razors will occasionally arrive with a package of old blades. Don't use them: the edges will be rough due to oxidation. Use only new blades that you've purchased.

When you buy a vintage razor, you frequently must clean it, and cleaning instructions are provided below. Some vendors, though, provide shave-ready razors, fully cleaned and sterilized.

Gillette

Tech

The Tech was made from 1939 through the 40's. It's a three-piece razor and gives a mild shave. In a poll of "best razor for a novice," the Tech came in third, just after the HD and the Super Speed. These are quite common and inexpensive on eBay.

Super Speed

The Super Speed is the second most recommended razor for a beginner. It is less aggressive than the HD and slightly more aggressive than the Tech. Some like this and some don't. It's a TTO (twist-to-open) razor: one piece with silo doors that open to admit a new blade.

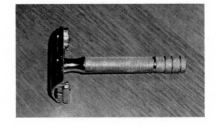

Aristocrat

Gillette used the name Aristocrat for several different razors, but the best (I think) is the 1940s version: a gold TTO razor, slightly more aggressive than the Super Speed. It's one of my favorites and is the razor shown on the cover of this book.

Fat Boy

The Fat Boy and the Slim Handle are two common Gillette adjustables. For both, the lowest setting is 1 and the highest (most aggressive) is 9. As with any adjustable, start at the lowest and least aggressive setting, and gradually increase the setting, day by day, until you get the shave you want. Some shavers like the Fat Boy, others prefer the Slim handle.

Slim Handle

Very like the Fat Boy, but with a longer and more slender handle. The head geometry is also different, so that the correct shaving angles for the two razors differ.

Lady Gillette

A long-handled, non-adjustable TTO razor designed for women. The handle comes in pink or blue or gold[78]. Although marketed to women, men also like the razor.

Wilkinson

Wilkinson is a British company, and the popularity of Wilkinson double-edged blades in the US is what prompted Gillette to move into making the first multiblade cartridge. Wilkinson continues to make double-edged blades, as well as shaving soap and shaving sticks.

The "Sticky"

The Wilkinson "Sticky" is an exceptionally attractive razor, and it won a number of design awards. In addition, it gives a terrific shave. They come up on eBay every now and then and are subject to fierce bidding. The name refers to the plastic handle which somehow doesn't get slippery even when it's wet.

Single-edge razors: Schick & GEM

Two other razor options I should mention, because they're both very nice razors: easy to use and offering a comfortable shave—and they apparently work well for those who tend to get razor bumps. Both use a *single-edged blade*, made of thicker steel than double-edged blades. These two single-edged razors are the Schick Injector[79] and the GEM G-Bar[80]. At the links, you'll find photos of the razors.

Schick razors come in various models[81]. I have a G8, a J1, and an M1, and all do a fine job with regular Schick blades. You can also try Ted Pella Teflon-coated injector blades[82].

The GEM also has several models, but the one I call the "G-Bar" (with a circled G on either side of the handle) seems to give a significantly better shave than the more common Gem Micromatic. Moreover, the G-Bar is usually available in excellent condition. Ted Pella Teflon-coated single-edged blades[83] work okay, but better are blades specifically made for shaving (Treet, PAL, and the GEM brands).

Both the Schick (or "Schick-Eversharp") Injector and the GEM G-Bar are easy to find on eBay and generally run less than Gillettes.

Cleaning your razors

If you pick up an old razor on eBay or at a flea market or the like, you may have to clean it before using it[84]. And your razor will also require cleaning from time to time as you use it. An easy schedule is to clean the razor whenever you put in a new blade.

My method to remove soap scum and hard-water deposits (until I got the ultrasonic cleaner—see below) was to soak the razor(s) for an afternoon in a solution of 4 parts warm water to 1 part white vinegar, then rinse, dry, and buff it. Use a *non-abrasive* cleanser (Bon Ami or Scrubbing Bubbles) and a toothbrush to do detailed cleaning.

Maas metal polish[85] does a good job—you use only a tiny amount. Using Maas with a toothbrush can clean the chequered handles quite well. After polishing the razor, be *sure* to wash off *all* the Maas before shaving: it burns newly shaved skin.

Barbicide works well. Immerse the razor for less than ten minutes—more may damage the plating—and then rinse the razor; or rinse the razor with a high-proof rubbing alcohol and let it air-dry.

A shaver on the forums noted[86] that boiling in a mix of vinegar and water works for Super Speeds, but this method with a Gillette adjustable will most likely turn the razor pink because of the reaction with the copper adjustment ring. So if you want to boil, use plain water (perhaps with some dishwashing detergent).

If the razor you get is gold-plated, the discussion groups advise against boiling it. They suggest instead letting it soak for a long time in warm water, then cleaning it with some soap-scum remover and a toothbrush. Boiling, they say, removes the lacquer that protects the gold plating.

If the razor shipped to you is not properly packed (in a sturdy box, for example), it can be bent during shipment. This happened to one razor I bought on eBay. So if the razor arrives only in a padded envelope, inspect it carefully—it may require a little corrective bending. If you buy a razor on eBay, you may want to request shipment in a box, well-padded.

The methods described above work well for routine cleaning, but a really good cleaning requires an ultrasonic cleaner. Good-quality ultrasonic cleaners are now available at relatively low cost.

The advice I received was to get a cleaner that's at least 50 watts. (Most ultrasonic cleaners for consumer use are 35 watts.)

I got the Kendal CD-4800, a 60-watt cleaner[87]. I didn't buy it from the store at the link (see endnote), but searched eBay for "ultrasonic" and found the same cleaner at a substantially lower price.

I fill the cleaning tank with tepid water from the tap, add a little dishwashing detergent and a splash of white vinegar (to dissolve hard-water deposits), and then run it for a minute to expel dissolved gases from the water. Then the razors go in for an 8-minute cycle. Sometimes I also find it necessary to use a little Maas polish to remove minor discolorations on smooth surfaces—e.g., the top of the razor.. The end result is a very clean razor, inside and out.

Do not use hot water in the cleaner: in some cleaners hot water weakens the bond between the ultrasonic transducer and the steel tank. If you know or suspect the razor is exceptionally dirty, soak it a while in hot water with dishwashing detergent before putting it into the cleaner.

The ultrasonic cleaner can be used to clean jewelry as well—except do not attempt to clean opals, pearls, emeralds, or any stone with a chip or crack: the ultrasonic cleaner can destroy those. The cleaner will not harm metal.

You can even use the ultrasonic cleaner to clean your shaving brush. Use a little vinegar in the water. Then dip the brush into the water and hold it by hand—don't put the whole brush including the knot into the water as this could loosen some bristles. Hold the handle about 1 cm above the water and run the cleaner for about 5 minutes on only the bristles.

In cleaning a secondhand razor, I don't believe that one needs to go to extremes of disinfection and sterilization. When you buy secondhand flatware, for example, you probably simply wash it before using it, with no other sterilization needed—even though other people have put the implements into their mouths. (Similarly, the flatware you use in a restaurant has not gone through any serious sterilization.) So no need to get carried away, in my opinion. A good washing in hot water, perhaps a dip into Barbicide or rubbing alcohol—it's hard for me to see that much more is required. (And I've already advised you not to use any old blade(s) that came with the razor—they are at best just collector's items.)

NINE

Shaving the stubble

USING a safety razor puts *you* in charge, and going from a multiblade cartridge to a safety razor is akin to going from an automatic transmission to a manual: you can get better performance by being more in control, but you must learn how to use it, practice your technique, and pay attention to what's going on.

One point before you actually pick up the razor and put blade to face: Some shavers have one or more moles in the shaving area, and sometimes a mole is shaped so that it's occasionally cut. If you have such a mole, I *highly* recommend that you get it removed. It's a simple procedure and a dermatologist can do it in an office visit. Not only does it make your shaving life better, it also removes a mole that, being on your face, is more or less constantly exposed to the sunlight.

Pressure

The first variable you must control is *pressure*. With the safety razor, you must **not** use pressure to try to get a closer shave: pressure must be *light*, the razor and the blade doing the work—exerting additional pressure will cause problems (cuts, razor burn, etc.). As described below, you obtain a closer shave with more passes, *not* more pressure.

Think of the razor as a little container of nitroglycerin and the head as a pressure switch. That should help.

To ensure light pressure, one shaver found that holding the very *tip*[88] of the razor handle with a two- or three-finger grip works well. This is intended as an instructional grip, not for daily use (at least not for me), but try it for at least part of a shave to demonstrate to yourself how a razor with a sharp blade works well even with very light pressure.

Probably the most common error for the novice shaver is incorrect pressure—and so far as I know, it is *never* having too light a pressure.

Using too much pressure can be a general problem, or it can be localized: on the right side of the face for right-handers, for example, or on the neck, often a problem area because of the various curves. Or it can appear only on the against-the-grain pass when the razor is held upside down.

Symptoms of the problem are razor burn (face red and hot), small nicks, razor bumps, and skin irritation. If you think you're using too much pressure, try "negative pressure": holding off some of the full weight of the razor. A sharp blade will cut fine so long as it's pulled along at the correct angle through the stubble. And *never* try to achieve a clean shave in one pass.

There are two reasons (I believe) for using too much pressure. First, getting a close shave with a multiblade cartridge requires pressure, so new safety-razor shavers who have used the multiblade cartridge are in the habit of pressing down. Indeed, some cartridge shavers, as the cartridge grows dull, continue to use it by exerting more pressure as they shave—a bad habit that causes serious problems when using a safety razor.

The second reason is that the shaver feels stubble when rinsing his face after the first pass and thinks he must not have used enough pressure. *Not so.* There *will* be stubble after the first pass—that's why you do multiple passes. The key is *progressive stubble reduction* over multiple passes: at least two, generally three, and sometimes four (explained below). Each pass leaves less stubble.

In particular, you want the stubble reduced as much as possible before you try an against-the-grain pass.

Blade angle

Besides pressure, the key variable in using the safety razor is *blade angle*. Try this: put the head of the razor against your cheek, the handle perpendicular to the cheek and parallel to the floor. Gradually bring the handle down toward the face as you make a shaving stroke, pulling the handle to drag the head down your cheek. When the handle's dropped roughly 30º from the initial perpendicular (depending on the razor you're using), the blade will make contact with the whiskers and begin to cut as you pull the razor.

That's the angle (more or less). The idea is that the edge of the blade is *cutting through* the whiskers, *not scraping over* them. If the room is quiet, you can hear the sound of the razor cutting through the whiskers. The idea is that you use the razor like a scythe, not like a hoe. Think of the blade as being almost parallel to the skin being shaved, encountering the stubble at almost a right angle.

In the left photo, the razor is being held at too steep an angle, and the blade is not cutting. In the center photo, the blade (bent over the hump of the platform) is close to parallel to the skin and is cutting through stubble. In the right photo, the handle is too low, so the blade is at too steep an angle and is scraping across the skin, producing razor burn.

Another image: think of the razor as a chain saw and the stubble as young saplings. You don't want to dig the chain saw into the ground (your skin), and you want it to cut through the saplings (stubble) more or less at right angles.

As the skin on your face curves this way and that—over the jawline, around the chin, and so on—you continually adjust the razor's angle, keeping the blade almost parallel to the skin being shaved.

Using short strokes enables you to focus on blade angle (and pressure) for the entire stroke—and for a short stroke the angle is likely to be constant. It helps to lock fingers and wrist, moving the razor with your arm: this makes it easier to maintain a constant angle.

The correct cutting angle is different for different razors, and you determine the correct angle through feel and the sound the blade makes as you shave. When I use my Gillette Super Speed, it's held flatter to the face than the Merkur Futur, for example. And with the Schick Injector and the Gem G-Bar, the cutting angle is when the razor's head is pretty much flat against the skin. You'll have to experiment to find the right cutting angle for each of your razors.

One shaver has pointed out[89] that the correct angle is extremely important. Use as little pressure as you like, but if the angle is too steep, the blade will dig in and cut. He said that none of the instructions on the Internet emphasize this point sufficiently. Consider it *emphasized.*

I have a tiny travel razor[90] with no handle: you in effect hold it by the head. On shaving with it, I discovered that the tactile feedback of holding the head told me immediately if I had stopped cutting cleanly and started scraping. One guy tried a similar approach[91] with a regular razor and found it helpful for getting the right feel.

So: hold the razor by the handle tip to feel the proper pressure, and hold it by the head to feel the proper angle. (These grips are for instructional purposes only—in your normal day-to-day shave, you won't hold the razor by either grip.)

Proper technique with the safety razor consists of using light pressure and the correct blade angle over your entire beard area, including the neck.

The grip

One shaver recently made an interesting discovery regarding how to hold a razor, though (like many good discoveries) it sounds obvious once you're told: hold the razor at the point of balance.

He points out that both the Futur and the Vision have a definite waist, unlike most razor handles, and both are heavier than the typical razor. He wondered whether the waist was designed to show the center of balance and the right place for the grip. For him (and me, as well), it works well: it's easier to control angle and pressure if you hold your razor at the point of balance. Give it a go.

When you grip the razor, your grip should be *light*, not tight.

Here we go

Recall the grain directions over your entire beard, referring if necessary to the diagram you made. Do your prep, pick up your razor, chant, "Light pressure, correct blade angle," and set to work on the first pass.

First pass: With the grain

Your first pass is *with* the grain (WTG). The second pass will be *across* the grain (XTG), either directly across or across at a slant. Those who do XTG at a slant usually do a second XTG pass on the opposite slant. Only the final pass will be against the grain (ATG), and in the beginning you should skip this pass, introducing it gradually as described below.

Use short strokes. With short strokes, you're more likely to use light pressure, keep the correct blade angle for the entire stroke, and keep your attention focused—all factors that make a good shave.

Of course, as with all dicta regarding shaving: Try it, and see how it works for you. But the long, sweeping strokes possible with a pivot-headed cartridge razor don't work well with the safety razor.

Move the razor with your arm—using the fingers or wrist tends to change the angle in the course of the stroke.

Stretching the skin where you're shaving can help lift the whiskers, and the taut skin is less likely to be cut. You can stretch the skin with your other hand (or, if your skin is too slippery for that, with a damp washcloth in your stretching hand) or, for the skin around your mouth, by grimacing. You shave away from the hand that's stretching the skin. The skin under the chin is easily stretched just by lifting your chin.

The upper lip is a tricky bit because of the unremovable nature of the nose. Fortunately, though, the nose is flexible, so with your free hand, you can push or pull the nose to one side and even upward to give your razor more room to work. You also can shave under the nose by coming in at a bit of a slant.

To stretch the skin of my upper lip, I simply draw my lip down over my teeth. Another guy pushes his tongue up between his front teeth and his lip. Still another puts a finger in his mouth and stretches his cheek to one side, pulling his upper lip tight. Do whatever works for you.

The Adam's apple presents a problem for some guys. One technique is to move that skin off to the side, so you can shave it without a big bump underneath it. Grip some neck skin between your fingers and pull to the side. Another trick is to swallow and hold it—that flattens the Adam's apple long enough for you to shave it. As you shave your neck, pay especially close attention to blade angle and to pressure and to the grain. The neck presents a tricky area in shaving.

The safety razor has two sides, and in shaving you flip back and forth, using both edges of the double-edged blade. Flip the razor over to the "clean side" after it's accumulated lather from a few strokes and then rinse it when both sides are covered in lather. After each rinse, give it a good shake—or two—to remove as much water from it as possible.

When you rinse your face after the first pass, you'll feel some stubble. That's fine. You will be doing another pass: the process is *progressive stubble reduction*. Each pass further reduces the stubble, and the end result is a smooth face.

Second pass: Across the grain

Once you complete the first (WTG) pass, rinse your face and re-lather (lather is always applied to a wet beard). The second pass is across the grain (XTG), and this will further reduce the stubble. The XTG pass is particularly useful for reducing the stubble on the upper lip, under the nose. In fact, I go both directions XTG on my upper lip and on my chin. The stubble there is particularly tough, and by minimizing it as much as possible, the ATG pass becomes much easier.

Again: light pressure, correct blade angle, and short strokes, with your attention focused on what you're doing.

Rinse, and—when you first start shaving with a safety razor—that's it. If you want further stubble reduction, you can re-lather after rinsing and do another XTG pass, going the other direction, but when you first start using the safety razor, *don't try ATG*, for two reasons.

First, until you master blade angle and pressure, ATG is likely to cause cuts and/or skin irritation. Second, in the ATG pass, you're holding the razor upside down, and you'll find it requires more practice and concentration to keep pressure and angle correct in that maneuver.

Third pass: Against the grain

When you are ready to shave ATG: rinse your beard before that pass and feel the stubble. The stubble should be almost gone—if it's not, do an XTG pass the other way. Before the ATG pass, you want the stubble truly minimized. If you are prone to getting razor bumps in some areas, skip those areas on the ATG pass.

When you first start doing ATG, re-lather your wet beard and do ATG *just on your cheeks.* That's the easiest area and will give you good practice without getting into the difficult curves and challenges of chin, jaw, neck, etc. After a few shaves, when you're happy with ATG on your cheeks and are comfortable with the ATG razor position, do your chin as well, then your upper lip, and finally your neck and under the jaw. Remember to keep a correct blade angle for the skin you're shaving, as the skin curves this way and that, and remember to use light pressure. Again: short strokes allow you to focus on angle and pressure for the entire stroke.

Enchante Online has a useful diagram[92] on the direction of the cutting strokes (assuming "normal" beard grain). I got a fine shave when I used some of this pattern, modifying it as dictated by my own beard. (For example, I used XTG on my upper lip.)

For a thorough shave, try a **four-pass shave**: WTG, XTG on a slant, XTG on the other slant, and ATG. You can modify the basic method[93] to suit the lineaments of your own face. The benefit of this method is how it progressively reduces the stubble so the final, ATG pass is quite comfortable.

Going for a clean, close shave in one pass results in too much pressure, a guarantee of razor burn and cuts—progressive reduction through multiple passes is the key.

I usually do a **three-pass shave**: WTG, XTG (ear-toward-nose), and ATG. As I mentioned, one small patch at the heel of my right jaw grows horizontally toward my chin, so with the usual three passes that particular patch never got an against-the-grain pass. So now my three passes include one little backward horizontal pass over that spot. And my ATG pass on my right cheek, near the mouth, tilts to match the grain pattern of my beard there.

As I mentioned, the beard on my chin and upper lip is particularly tough, so I do XTG both directions there—again, to reduce the stubble as much as possible before the ATG pass.

The polishing pass

Once you're doing the ATG pass, you can finish the shave with a polishing pass to remove the last traces of roughness. Do *not* do a polishing pass where you get razor bumps. There are three ways of doing the polishing pass: a water pass, an oil pass, ar a pre-shave pass.

The water pass

The water pass works well as a natural extension of the final (ATG) pass, especially if during the ATG pass you're using your non-razor hand to stretch the skin. After finishing that ATG pass, rub your face with your wet left hand.

When you find a rough patch, use "blade buffing" to remove it: keeping the proper angle and light pressure while doing extremely short ATG strokes, on the order of 1/4" or less, not lifting the blade as you move it back and forth. One shaver described the motion as if you were trying to scribble in a small section of your beard with a pencil. Blade buffing is one of the advanced shaving techniques[94] that experienced shavers use in the final passes.

Another advanced shaving technique, the J-hook, often works well on the neck. One shaver reported that he used the J-hook (a final-pass technique, remember), both clockwise and counterclockwise, and got a much smoother result with no irritation. Again: experiment.

The water from your hand, together with the residue of the lather, provides the lubricity, and because you are shaving with only water and whatever tiny bit of lather was left, the shave is naturally close enough to remove even very short stubble.

If little lather residue is left, squeeze the bristles of your shaving brush with the fingers of your left hand. Then as you feel for rough spots, you will apply a bit of lather to your face.

The left hand does double duty, both feeling for roughness and stretching the skin as needed, and if it's been doing that through the third pass, the transition to the water pass is seamless.

Although the water pass works well, I still find that I usually prefer the oil pass, which I find effective and pleasant.

The oil pass

In Method shaving, the final pass is a "touch-up" using Hydrolast Cutting Balm, which is a combination of oils and essential oils. The Cutting Balm pass works extremely well, so it's a natural step to try other oils. The idea is this: after you finish your regular shave—for me, a three-pass shave (with, across, and finally against the grain, lathering before each pass)—rinse well, apply a few drops of oil to the palm of your left hand (assuming you hold your razor in your right), rub it over your *wet* beard, and then do a "polishing" pass, feeling with your left hand for rough spots, then buffing those with the razor against the grain. Rinse, dry your face with a towel (which removes most of the oil, with the oil remaining acting as a skin conditioner), and apply aftershave of choice. If you want to use the alum block, use it after that final rinse.

Here's my current shave, step by step:
1. Wash beard with MR GLO.
2. Rinse. Lather. Pass 1 (WTG)
3. Rinse. Lather. Pass 2 (XTG), double pass on chin and lips.
4. Rinse. Lather. Pass 3 (ATG)
5. Rinse. Rub 2-5 drops oil on wet beard area. Do polishing pass.
6. Rinse. Towel dry.
7. Apply aftershave.

Commercial shave oils

I had superb results with the oil pass, so I experimented with different oils. Here's the list of commercial oils I've tried, almost all of which identify themselves as "pre-shave" oil. I, however, use them only for the oil pass. The list specifically does *not* including **Art of Shaving shave oil**—those who tried it said it was too thick and gummy and altogether unsatisfactory, so I skipped that one.

Hydrolast Cutting Balm[95] is one component of the Method shave, but certainly it can be used on its own. It's a "proprietary blend of vegetal oils, proprietary blend of essential oils." This was the origin of the idea, and thanks to Charles Roberts of Method shave fame. It's very nice: light fragrance, light oil, and does a great job.

Total Shaving Solution[96]: This oil seemed *very* mentholated, so it should appeal to menthol fans. Very slick, light, and does the job.

All Natural Shaving Oil[97]: Often called Pacific Shaving Oil since it's made by Pacific Shaving Company. This oil seems to have some emulsifiers which make it mix with the water, but it still provides an excellent surface for the oil pass. Though it lists menthol among the ingredients, the menthol was subdued and polite.

KingofShaves Kinexium ST Shaving Oil[98]: This one easily wins the prize for packaging: a little flip-top lid that hinges open, a press button that produces exactly the right amount. It does a good job, but the fragrance is somewhat off-putting—to me, it's like machine-oil.

Gessato Pre-Shave Oil[99]: This oil is light and clear and has no discernible fragrance, which in some ways is a benefit. Does a very nice job, but is somewhat pricey.

Rituals Skincare Pre-Shave Oil[100]: Very nice oil with a wonderful citrusy fragrance—orange, I thought, or perhaps grapefruit. Extremely pleasant: light oil, good protection, lovely fragrance. (As an aside, the Rituals Skincare Milk and Honey Lotion[101] is a wonderful aftershave balm. I like it a lot, and I'm not normally a balm guy.)

Oils from the supermarket

You can also use oils you find at the supermarket. All of those listed below are non-comedogenic oils[102]—that is, oils that have a very low probability of clogging pores. However, some people are more apt to get clogged pores than others, so you should (as always) be guided by your own experience.

All of the oils listed below have well established histories of cosmetic use and don't go rancid (as, say, flaxseed oil would). They are all listed as being good for the skin. And they are all good oils for cooking or salads, so they certainly don't have to be reserved exclusively for shaving—the oil pass requires very little oil, in any event, so you'll have plenty of oil left over for other uses.

- Almond oil
- Avocado oil
- Grapeseed oil
- Macadamia nut oil
- Olive oil

Leisureguy's Last-Pass Shaving Oil: I used a combination of the above to make an oil-pass mix. Alter the formula as you want—there's really nothing special about the mix I made, though it works for me. It is, however, thicker than the commercial oils listed above.

2 parts Almond oil

2 parts Avocado oil

2 parts Olive oil

1 part Grapeseed oil

1 part Macadamia nut oil

1-2 drops essential oil(s) (for fragrance)—as much as you want

It's important to add only *one* (1) drop of the essential oil and then try the mix—you can always add another drop if needed, but removing a drop is impossible.

Useful equivalences for making small batches: 2 Tablespoons = 1 fluid ounce, and 3 teaspoons = 1 Tablespoon. Knowing this, you can readily figure out how many ounces you'll make if you use regular measuring spoons: for example, if 1 part = 1 tsp, the above formula will result in 1 1/3 fl oz, plenty for a batch—that much will last you a long time. If 1 part = 1 Tbsp, the result is 4 fl oz (that is, 1/2 cup).

You could also pierce a few vitamin E capsules and add 2000 IU of vitamin E if you want. But several of the oils already contain vitamin E, so it's probably coals to Newcastle.

You can readily find plastic dispensers: for example this one[103] (natural) or this one[104] (cobalt blue). The "treatment pump" top (available in white or black) works just right to dispense a drop or two per push: exactly the right top for this application. If you buy one of the commercial oils in a larger container, you might want to decant an ounce into one of these little bottles with the treatment pump.

A shaver found that an organic massage oil, such as found in health food shops, works well for the oil pass. He uses an organic baby massage oil that consists of organic safflower, sunflower, avocado, grape seed, and almond oils, with olive leaf extract, tangerine and chamomile essential oils and vitamin C.

A suggestion from a shaver's wife: "Why not let the shave oil container sit in warm water while you shave?" Excellent idea.

The pre-shave pass

The commercial oils used for the polishing pass are mostly identified as "pre-shave" oils. And, as you might suspect, you can use other pre-shaves for a polishing pass: Proraso Pre- and Post-Shave Cream, PREP, or Crema 3P. Those are slick, provide protection, and sooth the skin.

Method Shaving

Charles Roberts of EnchanteOnline.com developed a method of shaving that some shavers really like. He uses some special supplies, and recommends the Merkur HD razor and a sharp blade. The special supplies consist of:

- The Shavemaster brush—or any large, fan-type brush
- An olive-oil soap, originally "The Cube" but now rounds
- A shaving paste used with the soap to produce the lather
- "Activator," a recent addition for lather production
- Cutting balm, discussed above
- Skin tonic and conditioner

A good introduction to Method shaving is provided by three videos made by Mantic[105]. The supplies listed above are available online[106].

My own experience with Method shaving was generally positive. Because the lather depends on the proportions of soap, shaving paste, and Activator, it does tend to vary somewhat from session to session, at least until you become skilled in doing the mix. The Shavemaster brush is large and works well to generate a lather from soap—if you have large hands, you're likely to be particularly appreciative of the brush. But, as noted, you can use any large brush.

Although I use Method shaving only occasionally, I do enjoy having it in my repertoire. If you're experimentally minded, you might want to give it a go.

TEN

The post-shave routine

AFTER you finish your shave, rinse your razor in hot water and stand it up to dry. If you're using a carbon-steel blade, rinse it in high-percentage rubbing alcohol (91% or higher)—the alcohol drives out the water and then quickly evaporates, leaving the blade dry so that it doesn't rust.

There's no need to remove the blade or even to loosen the razor's grip on the blade. In general, it's a good idea to minimize handling the blade: remove it only to discard it.

Rinse out your brush—first with warm water until the lather's gone, then with cold water. Shake it well, dry it on a towel if you want, then stand it on its base in the open to dry.

After you put the razor and brush away, rinse your face first with warm water and then with cold—quite refreshing.

The alum block

After the cold-water rinse and prior to using an aftershave, try using an alum block. It's extraordinarily refreshing, but something that (like coffee) appeals primarily to adults: the sensation you get is a tingling and sometimes a slight stinging. It's also an antiseptic, and could be beneficial for those who suffer from acne or other skin problems.

One good-sized alum block should last for a year or two (unless you drop it on a hard floor). According to Shavex, which makes the alum blocks sold by Mama Bear and Razor and Brush: "The Alum Block (for shaving and deodorant purposes) is usually Potash Alum. Potash Alum doesn't sting so much as Ammonium Alum, but some companies do use Ammonium Alum as a shaving block."

One inexpensive form of Potassium Alum (another name for Potash Alum) is some deodorant crystal sticks—for some reason these are often priced much less than the alum block sold to shavers. (Some deodorant sticks are, however, made with Ammonium Alum—so be sure to check.) The Wikipedia article on Alum provides more information.

Whether you use the alum block daily, weekly, or not at all will depend on how your skin reacts. Some find it works fine, others must use sparingly, and a few must avoid. If the alum block causes your skin to redden, like razor burn, you may be one of the unlucky few.

Glide the alum block over the freshly shaved part of your face while your face is still wet from the cold-water rinse. (No need to wet the block: just glide it over your wet face.) This is non-abrasive: the block simply slides over your freshly shaved face. The block is then placed on its little wooden rack to air-dry.

I have read where some have inexplicably attempted to use a styptic pencil as though it were an alum block, rubbing the side of the pencil on the face. This is misguided. The styptic pencil is not the same substance; it's usually aluminum sulfate anhydrous or titanium dioxide. Get a real alum block.

One shaver's use[107] is typical: he uses the alum block every day—not to stop nicks, but just for the pleasure and benefits: it's an antiseptic, reduces razor burn, stops minor bleeds, and provides feedback on how well he's shaved (less sting = better shave).

And the alum block has multiple uses. One woman notes[108] that the alum block seems to take care of pimples—she just washes her face with water and then glides the alum block over her wet face and follows that with Thayers Rose Petal Witch Hazel. The result: no pimples, and no residual powder from the alum block. (She says it also stops the stinging on bug bites.)

I let my alum-blocked face drip while I rinse my brush—first with hot water, then with cold—then shake it well and let it dry. My brushes dry standing on their base, which seems to work fine.

I then rinse my face again (rinsing after the alum block is important), dry it, and apply an aftershave. After that, if I have a nick or cut (nowadays rare), I use My Nik Is Sealed[109], a liquid styptic in a roll-on applicator. It works like a charm and is *much* better than a
78

styptic pencil—and it doesn't leave white deposits on your face. (The alum block won't stop bleeding from a cut—that's not its purpose.)

And that's it: the shave is complete.

Your technique will improve with each shave, so long as you're paying attention. Practice produces wondrous results.

Aftershaves

The shaving products previously mentioned—shaving brushes, shaving soaps and creams, double-edged blades, safety razors—have a somewhat limited market: men who have discovered the benefits of traditional wetshaving. The marketing dollars that create infinite new variations, and the advertising dollars that work to convince ~~gullible victims~~ potential customers of the wondrous benefits of the latest variation—even if it's only changing the color of the plastic in the razor's handle—are markedly absent for traditional wetshaving.

But now we reach aftershaves, and those products are sold to *every* shaver, so here you will find incredible variety. Badger & Blade has a lengthy review[110] that covers just some of the products available, sorted by skin type (dry, normal, combination, and oily).

Generally speaking, you can choose among an aftershave (bracing) or a balm (soothing) or a gel (moisturizing).

Many kinds of gel are available: Gillette gels, and also Anherb from India, Tabiano from Italy, and Arko from Turkey.

Thayers Witch Hazel is available at drugstores and health food stores and comes in a variety of fragrances[111], none of which linger. (Thayers has a sampler package[112] of their various witch hazels.) There's also a Thayers Witch Hazel Aftershave[113], a bit more bracing and an excellent aftershave if you're traveling, since it has no fragrance. (It's a 4-oz. bottle, but you'll be checking your shaving things anyway: blades, remember?)

Classic Shaving has a page with an entire array[114] of aftershaves—other vendors offer either a similar variety or various special blends.

Some that I've tried and liked: Taylor's No. 74, Mr. Taylor's, Dominica Bay Rum, Pashana, Geo. F. Trumper Spanish Leather, Geo. F. Trumper West Indian Extract of Limes Aftershave (with a wonderfully intense fresh lime fragrance), and the various types of Floïd aftershave. Pinaud Clubman has a nice old-timey fragrance. Some continue to swear by Old Spice, Mennen Skin Bracer, Barbasol, or Aqua Velva, which can be found at your local drugstore.

Some aftershaves are preparations specifically made to treat razor bumps. These are discussed in the following chapter on Skin Problems.

The artisanal soap makers—Em's Place, Honeybee Spa, Mama Bear, QED, Saint Charles Shave, and Tryphon—also make aftershave lotions and balms that are well worth trying. Appleton Barber Supply offers a great variety of aftershaves, including many old-time favorites. Booster's aftershaves[115], from Canada, are very nice—June Clover is a favorite.

If you want a balm as an aftershave treatment, look (at your drugstore, for example) for Neutrogena Razor Defense lotion, Triple Defense cream, or Nivea Aftershave Sensitive lotion. Also, there's Baxter of California Aftershave Balm, which you can get from QED (under "Other fabulous toiletry products" in the menu at the left of his Web site). You can also email him and other vendors for general recommendations regarding aftershave skincare. Barclay Crocker offers a very nice aftershave balm, as does Rituals Skincare.

Both Taylor of Old Bond Street's Luxury Herbal Aftershave Cream and the Geo. F. Trumper Skin Foods (Coral or Lime) are quite good aftershave balms. Proraso's pre- and after-shave cream[116] works well as an aftershave balm.

Aftershaves and colognes in retail stores have a high markup. If you want to explore further in this arena, take a look at on-line discounters such as FragranceNet.com or check for bargains on eBay.

ELEVEN

Skin problems

S OME shavers suffer specific skin problems: acne, razor bumps, and/or ingrown whiskers. And shavers who live in cold climates must also consider what winter's cold dry air (or the hot dry air inside buildings) does to their skin.

This chapter addresses those problems, but only up to a point. You should never assume that any medical advice from a layperson is accurate. Dermatologists go to school for many years for a reason: there's much to know, and new treatments and drugs are regularly developed. So what you learn in this section is not the final answer and may not even apply to your particular situation.

What I will explain are some suggestions from men who have tried various regimens and who are sharing what worked for them. It may or may not work for you because your skin, your general condition, your environment, and/or your problem may not correspond to their situation and their remedies. The same holds true for products mentioned: they work for some, but that doesn't mean that they will necessarily work for you.

For any of these conditions, shaving with a multiblade cartridge is a bad idea, even though multiblade cartridges are highly recommended by companies that make and sell them. But the tug-and-cut action of multiblade cartridges irritates the skin (bad for acne) and tugs out the whisker before cutting it (bad for razor bumps and ingrown whiskers).

Single-blade shaving—either with a safety razor using a single- or double-edged blade, or with a straight razor—is much kinder to your face once you have learned proper shaving techniques.

Acne

Acne is a skin problem that results from different causes, typically one (or a combination) of these:

- Excess sebum (an oily substance produced by certain cells)
- Rapid production of bacteria (which can live on the sebum)
- Skin cells shedding too quickly
- Inflammation resulting from the above

Acne can be mild[117], moderate[118], or severe[119] (endnotes include links that show photos). Mild acne can be treated at home, but moderate or severe acne is best treated with the care of a dermatologist. To see improvement once treatment begins may take as long as 4-8 weeks.

Note that your dermatologist may not be well-informed about shaving options and might, for example, recommend a multi-blade cartridge, which is strongly contraindicated.

Treatment of mild acne focuses on three things:

1. Avoiding skin irritation—avoid harsh scrubs, aggressive cleaning, rough brushes, strong soaps, and shaving with multiblade cartridges.
2. Keeping skin clean by gentle washing with a mild soap.
3. Applying preparations designed to treat acne.

Over-the-counter acne creams often contain benzoyl peroxide or salicylic acid. Benzoyl peroxide kills the bacteria that cause acne. Its principal side effect is excessive dryness of the skin, so don't use more than directed. Benzoyl peroxide also has a bleaching effect, and can affect hair, sheets, towels, and clothing.

Salicylic acid helps correct abnormal skin shedding and helps unclog pores, but has no effect on sebum production or bacteria. Salicylic acid may be irritating to your skin, so you may not be able to use it—the general rule is always to avoid skin irritation.

Sulfur-based compounds work well for some (although there's some research[120] that shows that acne returns with increased severity after using sulfur-based compounds). In addition to over-the-counter treatments, prescription medicines are available through your doctor or dermatologist.

There's more information at AcneNet[121], and Acne.org[122] describes a good regimen. In terms of shaving, that regimen requires some extension.

1. When you wash your face, do it gently, using only your hands and a mild soap or cleanser. Do not use a washcloth or scrubber. Cetaphil cleanser is recommended by many dermatologists.

2. Use a mild, unscented shaving soap or shaving cream, and a soft shaving brush rather than a "scrubby" one. Omega shaving brushes, for example, are quite soft and gentle, yet not floppy. Use the brush only to apply lather, rather than building the lather on your face.

3. Use very light pressure when shaving and maintain a good blade angle. If you cut a pimple, apply a topical antiseptic to the cut.

4. You may find that you cannot use a shaving oil, even though those discussed earlier have low comedogenicity[123]. You can try an oil, but if makes the acne worse, give it up.

5. After the shave, try using an alum bar, which is a mild antiseptic. Glide the bar gently over your skin after the cold-water rinse, let it sit for about half a minute, then rinse and pat your skin dry with a towel. Do not rub. (You might add this step each time you wash your face.)

6. Aftershaves or tonics containing alcohol may be too drying or irritating when used in combination with acne treatments. Try them and see whether they work for you.

7. Wait until your skin is fully dry before applying any acne treatments.

More detailed instructions, including timings and amounts, are available at the site, which also offers products to help with the acne.

The Mayo Clinic has a detailed series of articles[124] on acne, including information on causes and risk factors, when you should seek medical advice, and guidance on treatment, prevention, and self-care.

Razor bumps and ingrown whiskers

Razor bumps are caused when hair, cut close to the skin, curls as it grows and either curls under the skin without emerging or curls into the skin next to where it emerged. Either event irritates the skin, causing inflammation. In some cases, infection follows, which causes a sore and drainage. Men who are African, Mediterranean, Jewish, Nordic, or from other peoples who have naturally coarse or tightly curling hair often get 'razor bumps.'

The technical name is *Pseudofolliculitis Barbae*: "*pseudo*" (false) + "*follicle*" (hair) + "*itis*" (inflammation) + "*barbae*" (of the beard), often abbreviated as PFB. If the site becomes infected, "*pseudo*" no longer applies and the condition is called *Folliculitis Barbae* or "barber's rash." Photos of these conditions can be seen at the Dermatology Image Atlas[125].

Causes

The usual cause of PFB is shaving too closely. A multiblade cartridge, with its tug-and-cut action, is particularly bad: by tugging the whisker before it's cut, the cutting point is too close to the skin and can even be slightly beneath the skin's surface after the whisker pops back into place. But even a double-edged safety razor can deliver too close a shave, which leads to razor bumps. Electric razors, like multiblade cartridges, are particularly bad for men prone to PFB.

Shaving against the grain is a bad idea for the parts of your beard where you tend to get PFB, and stretching the skin as you shave there is equally bad. Both techniques are aimed at getting a closer shave, one source of the problem.

Another cause is irritation and damage to the skin from using a dull blade, or a sharp blade with bad technique, or an inadequate shaving preparation.

A common cause of infection is *Staphylococcus aureus* bacteria. The bacteria normally resides benignly in the nasal passages, but shaving can sometimes introduce it to hair follicles on the face. Once the hair follicle is infected, the result is redness, itching, and even small, pus-filled blisters. This is one of those things that vary by individual—I've never had such a problem, but some shavers are prone to such infection.

Cures

If you now have razor bumps, stop shaving for a few days or a week— let the whiskers lengthen, and with a sterile needle release any whiskers caught in the skin or beneath the skin. If you have infected sites, apply an antibiotic and let the sites heal. Benzoyl peroxide can help, but apply it sparingly since it can be irritating. It's a good idea to see your doctor or a dermatologist, who can help with the diagnosis and will possibly prescribe appropriate medication.

Prevention

Prevention has two parts. First is how you shave, and second are products specifically designed to prevent razor bumps.

Prep

Make sure that your preparation is thorough and excellent. You want the whiskers fully wetted so they will be more easily cut and less likely to be sharp at the cutting point.

Shave after you shower. Use a softening conditioner on your beard in the shower. Use ample amounts of warm water to soften the skin and whiskers before shaving.

Wash your beard at the sink, using a good pre-shave soap such as Musgo Real Glyce Lime Oil soap. Rinse and, leaving your beard wet, apply a wet, hot towel or washcloth to your beard for 3-5 minutes. You can apply lather to your wet beard before the hot towel/washcloth if you find that this increases the wetting action of the towel: just place the hot wet towel over your lathered beard.

After removing the towel, rinse your beard with hot water, and then use a technique suggested by Themba[126] on the ShaveMyFace forum. His suggestion is to use an Innomed Lice Comb[127]. (Moore Unique also makes a tool[128] for lifting the beard.)

The comb is quite fine. As you comb against the grain, use firm but comfortable pressure and a shallow angle (as if shaving with the comb). This lifts the stubble and removes ingrowns and dead skin.

Then make a good (thick, wet, dense) lather from a good shaving soap or shaving cream, and brush it on your wet and combed beard against your beard's grain.

Tools

Men who suffer from razor bumps say that the best razor to use is a straight razor. If you don't want to go that route, a single-edged razor—the Schick Injector or the GEM G-Bar, both readily available on eBay—is, they say, just about as good. A double-edged razor also works well provided that you do not attempt to shave too closely. The Bump Fighter Razor[129] with its special Bump Guard blades is also recommended by some, though it won't give a close shave.

Use a new blade for each shave (if your blade is inexpensive) or else sterilize the blade before you begin each shave by rinsing it in a sterilizing solution. You can use:

- rubbing alcohol (91% or higher); or
- a sterilizing product like Ritual Razor Rinse (easily found with a Google search) or Barbicide[130].

If you re-use the blade, make sure that it's sharp: discard it before it becomes dull.

Shaving

Consider shaving on alternate days, if that's possible for you.

Shave first the areas that don't have razor bumps, saving the bumpy areas for last so that the lather has longer to soften the hair.

Don't stretch your skin while shaving places that get razor bumps. Stretching your skin while you shave increases the chance that the whisker will 'snap back' to below skin level when it's cut.

Shave with the grain and possibly across the grain, but never against the grain in areas prone to razor bumps—do not try for a totally smooth (close) shave in those areas. (You probably can shave against the grain in places where you never have razor bumps.)

If you cut a bump, apply an antibiotic to prevent infection. You might try using an alum bar after the shave, since it's a mild antiseptic. Just glide it over your skin after the cold-water rinse. Let it sit for half a minute, then rinse, pat dry, and apply your shaving balm or aftershave or razor bump treatment. If the alum doesn't seem to work for you, discontinue using it.

Products

A number of over-the-counter products are specifically meant to prevent razor bumps. And through your doctor or dermatologist, you can get prescription medicines for the condition, such as eflornithine hydrochloride 13.9%, sold under the trade name Vaniqa. It's designed to remove facial hair for women, but it's apparently proven effective in controlling and treating razor bumps as well.

Following is a list of over-the-counter products. These—like many things in shaving—work for some, not for others. Posting questions in the shaving forums about any particular product will provide you information from those who have used it. It would be a good idea to do a forum search before posting the question, though, since you may well find threads discussing the product you're interested in. Common products[131] (links at the endnote):

Bump Fighter products (in particular the razor)
Bump Patrol
Dermagen Skin Revival System
Elicina Biological Treatment
Follique Treatment
High Time Bump Stopper Products
Moore Unique Skin Care
No Mo' Bumps Aftershave
Prince Reigns gel
Smart Shave Products
Tend Skin (you can make a version of Tend Skin at home[132])

Winter skin issues

Winter's cold, windy weather outdoors combined with hot, dry air indoors can adversely affect a shaver's skin. Look for soothing products that will treat your skin well. Examples: for shaving, Mitchell Wool-Fat Shaving Soap or a shea-butter soap from Honeybee Spa, Mama Bear, or Saint Charles Shave. Insitut Karité shaving soap, which is 25% shea butter, is good for your skin and produces an excellent lather.

Saint Charles Shave also offers a shea-butter shaving cream, or use Nancy Boy Shaving Cream—the Nancy Boy products in general are quite good for your skin. Institut Karité also makes shea butter shaving creams (20% and 25%).

For an aftershave, try l'Occitane or Institut Karité shea-butter balm, one of the Thayers witch hazels, or Geo. F. Trumper Coral (or Lime) Skin Food. One shaver recommends Nancy Boy Body Moisturizer (which, he says, is heavier and cheaper than the face moisturizer and works quite well).

Em's Place, Honeybee Spa, Mama Bear, QED, Saint Charles Shave, and Barclay Crocker all offer soothing and moisturizing aftershave lotions and balms that are well worth trying. With these small vendors, you can email or call them to ask about the specific problem you're facing and get their informed opinions on the best approaches and products for you.

TWELVE

Recommendation for a beginner shaving kit

ON ShaveMyFace.com Rob_TN has an excellent list of options for a beginner shaving kit[133] for someone on a limited budget (a student, for example). And Razor and Brush has ready-made shaving kits that run as low as $10.

Should the experiment not work out for you, you can readily find buyers for the equipment and supplies on the Buying/Selling forums on ShaveMyFace.com, BadgerandBlade.com, and TheShaveDen.com and on the Sales Board at RazorandBrush.com. Indeed, you might be able to get some of your equipment there—along with good advice. But before the recommendations, a couple of points.

Hair conditioner instead of lather?

Some have found that they can use hair conditioner in place of shaving soap or shaving cream: they wash their beard at the sink with soap and water, then rinse it and apply the hair conditioner to the wet beard. After each pass, rinse the beard and apply hair conditioner again before the next pass.

This doesn't work for everyone, but if it works for you, you won't need a shaving brush, shaving soap, or shaving cream—so it may be worth a try. "Not working" means either some skin reaction to the hair conditioner or razor burn (red, burning skin) because the hair conditioner is not providing enough protection from the blade.

I did try it, and at first it seemed great. But then I had a difficult time seeing where I had shaved (the hair conditioner makes a thin and transparent layer), and I did get bad razor burn. So I returned to the traditional shaving cream or soap.

Schick Injector as transitional razor

The Schick Injector (various models readily available on eBay, sometimes called the Schick Eversharp) offers a good transitional razor for those accustomed to shaving with a cartridge razor. (Note that the pre-1960 Schick models are noticeably more aggressive than the later models, which still provide an excellent shave.) The Schick has somewhat the same feel as a cartridge razor, but uses a single-edged blade—and the blades meant for shaving do a better job than the laboratory blades. The Schick (like the Gem G-Bar) is also a good razor for those who get razor bumps. However, for others I recommend the traditional safety razor with the double-edged blade.

Leisureguy beginner shaving kit

- Merkur Hefty Classic ("HD") (or another Merkur Classic)
- Blade sampler pack (the largest sampler pack)
- Edwin Jagger Best Badger brush (but see Rooney option below)
- A shaving cream (see choices below)
- A shaving stick and/or shaving soap (see choices below)
- Lathering bowl (deep cereal bowl—approx 5″ across, 3″ deep, with a hemispherical shape and a dark color)
- Glycerine (at health-food store or drugstore)
- One of the commercial shave oils or your own mix
- My Nik Is Sealed
- Alum block
- Aftershave (see choices below)

The above costs about the same as the price of 30 or so Fusion disposable cartridges. You might save a bit if you can find a Gillette Super Speed or Tech in good condition on eBay.

Although the Hefty Classic is recommended, you can substitute any of the Merkur Classics, since they all have the same head geometry. In particular, the Classic 1904 is a very nice little razor. I like it a lot. Or, if you want a larger handle, look at the Edwin Jagger line of safety razors[134], which use the Classic head.

If you tend to get razor bumps, consider the Bump Fighter razor[135], specifically designed to minimize razor bumps. It should be noted that this razor will not give a close shave, even on the parts of your face where you never get razor bumps.

Currently the largest sampler pack, with the greatest range of brands, is offered by Razor and Brush. Although you will initially be using only one brand, you will later want to explore, and the largest pack gives you the most chances of hitting the blade jackpot. If you live in the UK, you can get a sampler pack from Connaught Shaving (see Appendix). Again, I advise getting the largest pack. And pick up all the blades you can find in local stores to include in your testing.

Find in the pack a brand of blade that works reasonably well and stick with that brand for a couple of months before beginning to explore the sampler packs (as described in Chapter 7).

If you can afford it, I recommend that you get a Rooney Style 2 or Style 3 Small Super Silvertip brush instead of the Edwin Jagger Best Badger. The Rooneys are completely wonderful. Another option: the G.B. Kent BK4, a great brush.

I recommend that you get both a shaving cream and a shaving soap. You might as well practice with both from the start.

A popular choice for a first shaving cream is Proraso, an Italian shaving cream with a menthol-and-eucalyptus fragrance. However, some men's skin does not do well with the Proraso formula, especially in the winter months. So instead you might want to use Taylor of Old Bond Street Avocado Shaving cream, which has proved very popular with newbies. If you are allergic to fragrances, Truefitt & Hill Ultimate Comfort might be a good choice for a shaving cream.

For your first shaving soap, I recommend using a shaving stick, since lather production is easiest using a shave stick. (They can be found in unscented versions.) The D.R. Harris shave sticks produce a particularly good lather, or get a shave stick from Honeybee Spa and/or Mama Bear. The Arko shave stick ($2!) is excellent.

If you want to try soap in a tub, let me recommend QED's Special 218, or any of the Honeybee Spa or Mama Bear shaving soaps— those are made with shea butter and are quite nice to your skin. Both Honeybee Spa and Mama Bear soaps come in a wide variety of fragrances in addition to unscented versions. Or you might try a classic triple-milled shaving soap, such as Truefitt & Hill or D.R. Harris.

For an aftershave, Bay Rum is a classic fragrance, or you can use any of the various Thayers witch hazels if you want something soothing. Or you might prefer a moisturizing balm after you shave; Neutrogena Razor Defense is one such and is available at your local drugstore. Rituals Skincare Milk and Honey Lotion is a particularly nice aftershave balm.

For both equipment and supplies look in the Buying/Selling sections of the shaving forums. You often can find bargains there. You can post a "WTB" (Want To Buy) if you're looking for a specific item.

Your second razor

Regardless of your first razor, I recommend that your second razor be the Merkur Slant Bar. It should be a second razor because it requires a light touch and a sure hand, so you should gain experience in wielding a safety razor before using it. The Slant Bar with a sharp blade is the ideal tool if you have a thick, wiry beard and sensitive skin. It will not give closer shaves than the Vision, in my experience, but it's a different shave.

THIRTEEN

Sources of the most common problems

P ROBLEMS with the shave usually—though not always—have their cause in one of the following areas. If you have some problem in your shave that don't seem to stem from the causes listed below, the shaving forums (see appendix) are a good source of informed advice.

Insufficient Prep

Your beard must be fully wetted to soften—shave after showering, wash beard again at the sink with Musgo Real Glyce Lime Oil soap, and apply a good lather—dense and holding a substantial amount of water—to your wet beard. You can also try the hot towel treatment.

One sign of insufficient preparation—and, in particular, of a lather that's too dry and/or a lathering process that's too brief—is that the blade seems dull, pulling and tugging at the beard instead of cutting smoothly and easily. It may be, of course, that the blade *is* dull, particularly if you've been trying to avoid changing it. Or, if it's a new brand of blade, it may be either a bad blade or a brand that doesn't work for you.

But if you have a brand of blade that's been working well for you, and suddenly it doesn't seem to be cutting, suspect the prep. Make sure the lather's wet enough, and spend a good amount of time with the brush, working the lather over and into your beard. Begin your shave with the softest part of your beard, leaving the toughest (usually the chin and upper lip) for last so that those whiskers have more time to soak in the lather and thus soften.

Wrong Blade for You

Blade selection is crucial. Novices focus on the razor, but the razor is just a device for holding the blade and presenting the edge at the correct angle to the stubble. Different people require different blades. Get a sampler pack so you can find the best blade for you. This step is absolutely essential if you want close and comfortable shaves. Don't skip it. And you *cannot* rely on recommendations from other shavers: one man's pebble is another man's pearl, and vice versa. This is enormously difficult to grasp—if you have a terrible shave with a blade, it's hard to believe that others would actually *like* the blade, and vice versa. And yet it's true: *every* blade has those who like it and those who hate it. And until you try the blade, you don't know into which group you fall.

Incorrect Blade Angle

Blade angle is absolutely critical. The blade should be *almost* parallel to the skin being shaved, so that the blade's edge strikes the stubble almost at a right angle as the blade slides along your skin.

Where the skin has a lot of curves (for example, jawline, neck, chin), you have to maneuver the razor a fair amount to keep the blade angle correct because the safety razor, unlike the cartridge razor, does not pivot. Making short strokes helps you stay focused on blade angle.

No matter how light the pressure, if the angle's wrong, you'll nick or cut yourself.

Too Much Pressure

Use very light pressure. Shaving with a cartridge either requires or encourages pressure, so this is a habit that cartridge shavers must unlearn. Often the weight of the razor by itself is enough to cut the stubble. Hold the blade to minimize pressure—for example, by the balance point on the handle. When you rinse after the first pass, you'll feel quite a bit of stubble. This does **not** mean you should use more pressure—in single-blade shaving, you eliminate stubble by progressively reducing it over 2, 3, or 4 passes.

Keep the pressure light. Your face will thank you.

Ignoring Your Beard's Grain

It's vital that you know the direction of your beard's growth, since the sequence of passes is first *with* the grain, then *across* the grain, and then (if stubble is sufficiently reduced and you don't have to be concerned about razor bumps) *against* the grain. (If too much stubble remains for a comfortable against-the-grain pass, first shave across the grain the other way.)

Generally, the beard on your face will grow downward—but not always. I have a couple of patches where it grows more or less sideways. The grain on the neck can be anything. To find the grain, wait 12-24 hours after you've shaved, then rub your face and neck. The direction that's roughest is against the grain. You'll find the "roughest" direction is different on different parts of your face and neck.

Setting an Adjustable Razor Too High

Some novices inexplicably dial their adjustable razor to the most aggressive settings—4, 5, or 6 on the Futur or Progress, or 8 or 9 on the Gillette Adjustable—and then find themselves staring in the mirror at their lacerated face. With adjustables, start with the *lowest* setting (1 on Futur or Progress, 2 or 3 on Gillette Adjustable), and advance the setting only as you must in order to get a good shave. As soon as you get a good shave, stop there. You want the lowest setting that works, not the highest setting you can stand. It's not a contest.

—

If you pay attention to these basic points, you'll enjoy your shaves. There will be a learning curve, as you make the transition from cognitive understanding to practiced skill, but you will at least know what you're trying for.

FOURTEEN

Where to get more information

NOW that you're at the end of this introductory book, you may well want to know more.

A write-up on MSNBC[136] on how to get the perfect shave covers some of the same points as this book.

A commenter on my original post on shaving pointed out a "how-to-use" guide[137].

I've mentioned the series of videos[138] made by Mantic, which offer an introduction to and demonstration of many of the topics covered above.

The wetshaving forums—Badger & Blade, ShaveMyFace, The Shave Den, and The Wetshavers Group—offer invaluable advice to novices and allow you to post your own questions. You will get a range of views and advice, which is all to the good: shaving solutions vary by person, so knowing a range of solutions is quite helpful. In addition to the forums, Razor and Brush's message board is a very good place to post questions and get answers.

One benefit of using these forums is that, when you describe a problem you're facing, you will often get responses from men who have faced (and solved) the identical problem, and thus you can profit from their experience.

Some manufacturers of shaving products offer free samples, which are quite useful. For example, a sample is more than enough to test for any special sensitivity or allergy: just rub a bit inside your forearm and let it sit. If your skin reacts adversely, it's probably not a good product for your face. On ShaveMyFace you can find a comprehensive list[139] of sources of samples.

Finally, the best source of information is your own experience and tests and observations and reflection.

If you are wondering whether your lather is sufficiently wet— or too wet—the best course is to experiment: try using less water, then using more water, and see how it works for you.

If you are wondering whether a particular pre-shave you have really works, or whether it works better if you apply it before each pass, experiment. Shave a week with it, followed by a week without. Try a week of using it only before the first pass, followed by a week of using it before every pass.

Thoughtful experimentation and close observation of outcomes are, in shaving as in science and life in general, the most reliable source of knowledge.

Go now and experiment.

Appendix

Links are also available at http://tinyurl.com/4rt6nf in clickable form. Links are organized by category:

1. Forums
2. Reference
3. Vendors
4. Book links (by endnote number)

Forums

Badger & Blade – www.BadgerandBlade.com
Men Essentials Shaving – http://tinyurl.com/yvxsuq
Razor and Brush message board - http://tinyurl.com/2hj8db
ShaveMyFace – www.ShaveMyFace.com
Straight Razor Place – www.StraightRazorPlace.com
The Shave Den – www.TheShaveDen.com
Wetshavers Group - http://tinyurl.com/2dlvsl

Reference

Blade widths and the effects - http://tinyurl.com/5yusmq
Gillette date codes - http://tinyurl.com/k9g2n
Museum of safety razors - http://tinyurl.com/3yzsm2
Mantic's shaving videos - http://tinyurl.com/y2fx33
Schick Injectors - http://tinyurl.com/27vor9
Shaving information – www.shaveinfo.com
Shaving product samples - http://tinyurl.com/2gwu8c

Vendors

Following is a list of on-line vendors for the wetshaving community. This list is volatile, as new vendors come on-line, so be sure to also check the supplemental post.

* = complete vendor (shaving brushes, soaps, creams, razors, blades, aftershaves)

H = handmade shaving soap, creams, lotions, aftershaves, etc.

C = will accept calls from men seeking product advice

Appleton Barber Supply - http://tinyurl.com/2xntk4 - 800-236-0456 Central Time - info@appletonbarbersupply.com - Primarily of interest for great selection of aftershaves (at link).

Art of Shaving - www.theartofshaving.com - 800-696-4999 Eastern Time - AOS shaving cream and soap and aftershave, Merkur. (Shave oil not recommended: too gummy)

Atkinson's - http://tinyurl.com/2dc6zy - info@atkinsonsofvancouver.com - 604-736-3368 800-803-0233 Pacific Time - Plisson brushes.

Auravita – http://tinyurl.com/269cqd - A general supplier in the UK, patronized by wetshavers mainly as a source of Swedish Gillette blades (at the link), though they do carry, for example, Kent shaving brushes.

Barber Depot, Inc. - http://tinyurl.com/3zu2ha - barberdepot@verizon.net - 877-292-0100 Eastern Time - Mainly of interest for the Astra Superior Platinum blades: $11/100.

Barbieria Italiana – See Tryphon Barbieria Italiana

H* **Barclay Crocker** – http://barclaycrocker.com – sales@barclaycrocker.com – 800-536-1866 - Many brands of Bay Rum, Merkur, Proraso, Musgo Real (including Glyce Lime Oil pre-shave soap), Geo. F Trumper, Truefitt & Hill, Taylor of Old Bond St, Col Conk, Woods of Windsor, Shave Brushes & Mugs, Barclay Crocker Custom Scenting.

Bon Savon - http://tinyurl.com/2a67rx - info@bonsavon.com – 877-832-4635 Pacific Time - Provence Santé, Pre de Provence, Swedish Summer Soap, Lightfoot's Shaving Soap.

Carbolic Soap Co. – http://tinyurl.com/yucvfb - Mitchell's Wool Fat Shaving Soap (best price).

CH* **Classic Shaving** – www.classicshaving.com – info@classicshaving.com – 760-288-4178 Pacific Time Cremo Cream, Dovo, Feather, Merkur, Proraso, Rooney, Taylor of Old Bond Street, Thiers-Issard, Truefitt & Hill, Vulfix, Zowada.

* **The Classic Shaving Store** – http://tinyurl.com/226nwy – Col. Conk, D.R. Harris, Merkur, Musgo Real, Simpsons, Gillette (vintage). An eBay store.

H* **Connaught Shaving** - http://tinyurl.com/2gl8cb - info@suffolksupplies.co.uk - 07963 325842 - Carter & Bond, Derby, Gillette, Merkur, Parker, Proraso, Treet. Offers a blade sampler pack: http://tinyurl.com/yr36v2

Cotton Blossom Crafts – http://tinyurl.com/ysb3oh - DeLong, Weishi razors.

Crabtree & Evelyn - http://tinyurl.com/2ckbjk - 800-272-2873 Eastern Time - Edwin Jagger, C&E Shaving creams and soaps and aftershave.

eBarbershop - http://tinyurl.com/22du5u - sales@eBarbershop.com – Col. Conk, Crabtree & Evelyn, G. B. Kent, Merkur, Personna, Pinaud, Woods of Windsor.

eBay - Safety razors and blades – http://tinyurl.com/2hj626
At the link is a list of eBay offerings, including bulk-purchase Israeli and Derby blades, safety razors of all kinds, and the like. List sorted by newly listed, but can be resorted to find auctions ending soonest.

H* **Em's Place** – www.emsplace.com and www.shaveinfo.com – emily@emsplace.com – Dovo, Em's (shaving soaps and creams, aftershaves, lotions), Geo. F. Trumper, Gold Dachs, Merkur, Omega, Proraso, Simpsons, Speick, Tabac, My Nik Is Sealed.

HC* **Enchante Online** - www.enchanteonline.com - enchantetx@sbcglobal.net - 888-220-2927 Central Time Derby, D.R. Harris, Feather, Geo. F. Trumper, Israeli Personna, Merkur, Shavemaster, Taylor of Old Bond Street, Wilkinson.

* **The English Shaving Company** - www.theenglishshavingcompany.com - D.R. Harris, Edwin Jagger, Geo. F. Trumper, Proraso, Swedish Gillette blades.

* **Executive Shaving Company** - www.executive-shaving.co.uk - Cyril R. Salter, Dovo, D.R. Harris, Edwin Jagger, Geo. F. Trumper, Rooney, Merkur, Taylor of Old Bond Street, Thiers Issard, Truefitt & Hill.

* **Fendrihan** – www.fendrihan.com - info@fendrihan.com - 905-230-1254 Eastern time. Col. Conk, Derby, D. R. Harris, Gold Dachs, J.M.

Fraser, Merkur, Musgo Real, Simpsons, Taylor of Old Bond Street, Valobra, Vulfix, Kent shaving soap (same as Mitchell's Wool Fat)

The Frenchy Bee - http://tinyurl.com/2gd3l7 - 866-379-9975 Pacific Time, closed weekends. Durance L'òme shaving soap and aftershave, Institut Karité, Pré de Provence, Roger & Gallet, et al.

G. B. Kent & Sons - http://tinyurl.com/4ftyn8 - +44(0)1442-232623 - vjp@kentbrushes.com - G.B. Kent shaving brushes (and hair brushes), Kent shaving cream and shaving soap (shaving soap is the same as Mitchell's Wool Fat Shaving Soap).

H **The Gentleman's Quarter** - http://tinyurl.com/4go42u (PDF) thegentlemensquarter@verizon.net - Handmade shaving soaps and creams in unusual fragrances. Web site planned.

The Gentlemens Refinery – www.thegr.com – 866-444-7428 Mountain Time. Excellent shaving creams, aftershave balms, shave oil, shaving brushes. Products manufactured by a fourth-generation barber.

* **The Gentlemen's Shop** - www.gentlemans-shop.com - sales@gentlemans-shop.com - 01488 683536 / 684363 (UK) - Art of Shaving, Castle Forbes, Dovo, D.R. Harris, Edwin Jagger, G.B. Kent, Geo. F. Trumper, Merkur, Rooney, Simpsons, Taylor of Old Bond Street, Truefitt & Hill.

H **Honeybee Spa Soaps** – http://tinyurl.com/yctaxw
Handmade shea butter shaving soaps and shaving sticks, along with broad line of handmade creams, lotions, shampoos, and other toiletries. Wide variety of fragrances.

C* **Lee's Razors** – www.leesrazors.com – leesrazors@aol.com - 800-503-5001 Eastern Time - Col. Conk, Derby, Dovo, Feather, Geo. F. Trumper, Merkur, Mitchell's Wool Fat Shaving Soap, Musgo Real (including Glyce Lime Oil soap), Proraso, Simpsons, Vulfix.

London's Bathecary - www.shoplondons.com -
434-220-0540 Eastern Time - Caswell Massey, Floris London, Geo. F. Trumper, Lightfoot's, Mitchell's Wool Fat Shaving Soap, Penhaligon's, Taylor of Old Bond Street.

H **Mama Bear** - www.bear-haven.com - sclark@core.com
Full line of handmade shaving soap, shaving stick, shaving cream, aftershaves, along with regular soaps. Wide variety of fragrances. Also containers (make your own shave stick), alum block.

102

* **Men Essentials** - www.menessentials.com –
877-449-6599 Eastern Time - Acca Kappa, Art of Shaving, Baxter of
California, Col. Conk, Merkur, Truefitt & Hill.

* **Momentum Grooming** - http://tinyurl.com/4xwulp - 604-689-4636;
1-877-886-4636 Pacific Time (Vancouver BC) - Merkur, Musgo Real,
Proraso, True Gentleman, Truefitt & Hill

Moss Scuttle – www.sarabonnymanpottery.com -
902-657-3215 Atlantic Time - The famous Moss Scuttle along with
a wide variety of pottery and hooked rugs.

* **Mühle-Pinsel** - http://tinyurl.com/yu3zze -
info@muehle-shaving.com - German company. Baxter of California,
D.R. Harris, Edwin Jagger, Geo. F. Trumper, Mühle-Pinsel, Proraso.

* **Nashville Knife Shop** – www.nashvilleknifeshop.com -
info@nashvilleknifeshop.com – 812-988-9800 Central Time - Col.
Conk, Cremo Cream, Derby, Dovo, D.R. Harris, Merkur, Proraso,
Mühle-Pinsel.

Nancy Boy - www.nancyboy.com – contact@nancyboy.com - 888-746-
2629 Pacific Time - Nancy Boy products, good for sensitive skin.

l'Occitane - http://tinyurl.com/q425c - 888-623-2880
Cade line of shaving soap, cream, shea butter aftershave balm.

H **Olivia Shaving Soaps** - http://tinyurl.com/2hxzey
Handmade shaving soaps and creams; Crema Sapone Cella.

Pacific Shaving Company - http://pacificshaving.com/ - Shaving oil,
liquid styptic.

The Perfect Shave - http://www.theperfectshave.co.uk/ -
info@theperfectshave.co.uk - Art of Shaving, Castle Forbes, Edwin
Jagger, Merkur, Parker, Geo. F. Trumper, Truefitt & Hill.

CH* **QED** – www.qedusa.com - qed@quod.com
401-433-4045 Eastern Time - Castle Forbes, Cyril R. Salter, Geo. F.
Trumper, Merkur, Musgo Real, Omega, QEDman (his own line of
soaps and lotions), Proraso, Savile Row, Taylor of Old Bond Street,
Truefitt & Hill.

Razor and Brush – www.razorandbrush.com - Has articles, history of
shaving, book reviews, links to message board, sales board, various
shave blogs and sites, and to Barbieria Italiana, the store. See also
Tryphon Barbieria Italiana below.

Retrorazor – www.retrorazor.com - chaddmbennett@retrorazor.com
Derby, Weishi, starter gift-packs, shaving workshops in Seattle

H **Rituals Skincare** – www.ritualsskincare.com 503-722-1400 Pacific
Time - linda@ritualsskincare.com – Pre-shave oil, shaving cream
(more like a soap), synthetic-bristle shaving brush, and
(particularly recommended) Organic Milk and Honey Lotion with
Tamanu Oil — very nice indeed. Other bath and skin products.

H **Saint Charles Shave** - www.saintcharlesshave.com
sue@saintcharlesshave.com - Handmade shaving soaps, creams,
aftershaves, lotions, eau de toilettes.

* **Sesto Sento** - www.sesto-sento.com - info@sesto-senso.com - 301-
668-5018 - Castle Forbes, Geo. F. Trumper, Merkur, Musgo Real
(including Glyce Lime-Oil Soap), Omega, Pashana, Proraso, QED
Shaving Sticks, Savile Row brushes, Taylor of Old Bond Street,
Truefitt & Hill, Vulfix shaving cream.

Shave Center of the Internet - www.shavingsupplies.com
Altesse, Col. Conk, Dovo, Merkur, Thiers Issard.

The Shave Den Store - http://tinyurl.com/4y7mex - part of The Shave
Den Forum. Selection of shaving soaps and creams, both with
fragrance oils and essential oils, along with aftershaves, colognes,
and the like.

Shavemac - www.shavemac.com - info@shavemac.de - Dovo, Haslinger,
Merkur, Olivesoap, Shavemac, Speick, Tabac, Weleda.

Shaving Essentials, LLC - www.shavingessentials.net -
shavingessentials@gmail.com - 859-230-8563 – Booster, Col. Conk,
D.R. Harris, Geo. F. Trumper, J.M. Fraser Shaving Cream, Merkur,
Mitchell's Wool Fat, Royall fragrances, Yardley.

ShavingStuff.com - www.shavingstuff.com - Not a vendor, but a site
that routinely reviews shaving equipment and supplies, from time
to time finding things of interest to traditional wetshavers.

* **Smallflower** – www.smallflower.com - Voice 800-252-0275 Central
time - fax 773-989-8108 - Geo. F. Trumper, Mitchell's Wool Fat,
Muhle Pinsel, Musgo Real (including Glyce Lime Oil pre-shave
soap), Pre de Provence, Provence Santé, Proraso, Speick, Tabac.

Superior Brushes - www.superiorbrushes.com -
admin@superiorbrushes.com - Custom-made shaving brushes with

knots 20mm, 22mm, 25mm, 30mm. You specify handle color and shape as well as the knot you want.

Thomas Anthony Company - http://tinyurl.com/2g8utv
Custom wooden-handled shaving brushes.

* **Tones Barber Shop** -www.tonesbarbershop.co.uk -
Col. Conk, Cyril R. Salter, Dovo, London Shaving Co., Merkur, Taylor of Old Bond Street, Tones Barber Shop.

H* **Tryphon Barbieria Italiana** - http://tinyurl.com/2gzaeg -
tryphon@tryphon.it – Offers a wide variety of blades: Astra, Dorco, Dura, Feather, Sputnik, Treet, Wilkinson; also Arko, Floïd, Royall aftershaves, Proraso, Institut Karité, Valobra shaving soaps, and others. Sells a wide range of sampler packs of blades and also beginner shaving kits (brush, soap, razor, blades, etc.).

Tulumba - http://tinyurl.com/283vbt - info@tulumba.com
866-885-8622 Eastern Time - Arko, alum block.

C* **Vintage Blades LLC** - www.vintagebladesllc.com -
jim@vintagebladesllc.com - 410-357-8055 Eastern Time
Col. Conk, D. R. Harris, Dovo, Floris London, Merkur, Rooney, Shavemac, Thayers, Taylor of Old Bond Street, Truefitt & Hill, Vulfix.

C* **The Well Shaved Gentleman** - thewellshavedgentleman.com -
443-717-3969 Eastern Time - Shave-ready Dovo straight razors, strops and hones. Provides excellent advice on straight razors.

West Coast Shaving – www.westcoastshaving.com
Sells sampler packs of blades as well as Swedish Gillette and made-in-England Wilkinson Sword.

---

[1] Skin care: See http://tinyurl.com/2pttmv

[2] Flow: See http://tinyurl.com/a5f4s. Each person can find tasks appropriate for him or her that will promote flow: rock climbing, painting or drawing, gardening, cooking, and the like. Mihaly Csikszentmihalyi defined the term in his studies and in the book that emerged from them, *Flow: The Psychology of Optimal Experience*. See http://tinyurl.com/ywzrea

[3] Cognitive dissonance: See http://tinyurl.com/boyuz

[4] Ben Franklin was familiar with the effect if not the term. He decided to win over an opponent in the Pennsylvania state legislature:

> I did not ... aim at gaining his favour by paying any servile respect to him but, after some time, took this other method. Having heard that he had in his library a certain very scarce and curious book I wrote a note to him expressing my desire of perusing that book and requesting he would do me the favour of lending it to me for a few days. He sent it immediately and I returned it in about a week with another note expressing strongly my sense of the favour. When we next met in the House he spoke to me (which he had never done before), and with great civility; and he ever after manifested a readiness to serve me on all occasions, so that we became great friends and our friendship continued to his death. This is another instance of the truth of an old maxim I had learned, which says, "He that has once done you a kindness will be more ready to do you another than he whom you yourself has obliged."

In terms of modern psychology, the opponent observed himself doing a favor for Franklin, a favor that Franklin framed as a great favor, and reduced his cognitive dissonance by deciding that he must like Franklin after all.

[5] Wilkinson technology: See http://tinyurl.com/2gce5h#218644

[6] Report at http://tinyurl.com/2ba4er#133588

[7] "What was I thinking?": See http://tinyurl.com/2a4rm3

[8] eBay safety razors: See http://tinyurl.com/5n4l3g

[9] For a wonderful account of the first-time experience, read what brderj and DEsquire say in the thread: http://tinyurl.com/2aln4w.

[10] Series of videos made by Mantic: See http://tinyurl.com/y2fx33

[11] Different types: See http://tinyurl.com/ytfhfn

[12] A cream: See http://tinyurl.com/yr8kn5

[13] The Art of the Straight-Razor Shave: See http://tinyurl.com/2c4zuz

[14] 100% glycerine: See http://tinyurl.com/29d2fr

[15] From a comment: See http://tinyurl.com/2ctjw6

[16] Hydrosol: Herbal distillates are aqueous solutions or colloidal suspensions (hydrosols) of essential oils usually obtained by steam

distillation from aromatic plants or herbs. These herbal distillates have uses as flavorings, medicine and in skin care. Herbal distillates go by many other names including floral waters, *hydrosols*, hydrolates, herbal waters, toilet waters, aqua vitae, and essential water. See also http://tinyurl.com/2e57ae

[17] Several grades: See http://tinyurl.com/23vwkc

[18] Synthetic bristles: See http://tinyurl.com/22r92w

[19] Made by hand: See http://tinyurl.com/2y4wev

[20] Make your own: See http://tinyurl.com/rbwjd - scroll down

[21] Clear differences: See http://tinyurl.com/yow8zh

[22] Vulfix brushes: See http://tinyurl.com/8bkbu

[23] Simpson brushes: See http://tinyurl.com/24ntes, http://tinyurl.com/ywt35u, and http://tinyurl.com/yopp63

[24] Rooney brushes: See http://tinyurl.com/35b9ws and http://tinyurl.com/yrmm8k

[25] Simpson measurements: See http://tinyurl.com/24kuln

[26] Omega brushes: See http://tinyurl.com/yrdzbu and http://tinyurl.com/3ezbxq

[27] Omega brush measurements: See http://tinyurl.com/2c6pad

[28] Shavemac brushes: See http://tinyurl.com/2xayv8

[29] Kent brushes: See http://tinyurl.com/g8zyf (also has Rooney and Edwin Jagger brushes). The BK4 is the best size.

[30] Superior Brushes: See http://tinyurl.com/2dy5uy

[31] Crabtree & Evelyn Edwin Jagger Best Badger brush: See http://tinyurl.com/2fjtb6

[32] English Shaving Co. Jagger Best Badger brushes: See http://tinyurl.com/yp3upw

[33] Wooden-handled brushes: See http://tinyurl.com/22prko

[34] Shaving brush innovations: See http://tinyurl.com/22xrfs

[35] One video: See http://tinyurl.com/yvfjjf

[36] Some nice accessories: See http://tinyurl.com/2bnqoe

[37] Anatomy of hairshaft: See http://tinyurl.com/3elobn

[38] Stand for the brush: See http://tinyurl.com/2gl5lj

[39] Brush cleaning: See http://tinyurl.com/yvg3hg and also the videos at http://tinyurl.com/yvmfr6

[40] M.A.C. brush cleaner: See http://tinyurl.com/25dj7o

[41] Sunbeam Hot Shot: See http://tinyurl.com/yqxzng

[42] Zojirushi hot-water dispenser: See http://tinyurl.com/2gkf6b

[43] UtiliTEA kettle: See http://tinyurl.com/e226e

[44] Somewhat drier: See http://tinyurl.com/23cop2

[45] Video referenced above: See http://tinyurl.com/yvfjjf

[46] Mantic video: See http://tinyurl.com/y2fx33

[47] More information: See http://tinyurl.com/2cbkvo

[48] Problem with lather: See http://tinyurl.com/yusrqk

[49] Moss Scuttle: See http://tinyurl.com/27ultr

[50] Dr. Moss quotation: http://tinyurl.com/ytfqz3

[51] Georgetown Pottery: http://tinyurl.com/3twdjw
Georgetown Scuttle: http://tinyurl.com/4jo4uj

[52] J.M. Fraser shaving cream: See http://tinyurl.com/5uk7oq

[53] High praise: See http://tinyurl.com/2zp35v

[54] An illustrated guide: See http://tinyurl.com/29zlku

[55] Mitchell's Wool Fat Shaving Soap: See http://tinyurl.com/yucvfb

[56] Tabac soap: See http://tinyurl.com/2hzk8r#tabac

[57] Rivivage: See http://tinyurl.com/5d2ny4; a three-pack is available at
http://tinyurl.com/6cbn4o

[58] Virgilio Valobra soap: See http://tinyurl.com/2c6pat

[59] Durance L'òme soap: See http://tinyurl.com/5ef9hk

[60] Honeybee Spa now sells shaving sticks, but I'll include instructions
on how to make a shaving stick from a Honeybee Spa soap or any
glycerine soap. (This will *not* work with triple-milled soaps.) First, get
a shaving stick container (e.g., from Bear-Haven.com). Then put the
glycerine soap in a Pyrex measuring cup, and put that in a pan of hot
water. Heat the pan of water over low heat until it's 150ºF, then turn
off the burner and leave it for a while. (The soap takes a while to
melt.) You may have to reheat the water, but no need to go over 150º.
(Patience helps.) While waiting for the soap to melt, turn the pusher
of the container so that it's at the bottom. Do not lubricate the
container—and in particular, do **not** use silicone grease—it will
waterproof your brush and kill the lather. See
http://tinyurl.com/22x8r7#250052 for more on this. When the soap

has melted, pour it into the container and wait until it's cooled. Voilà! Your own shaving stick. If it does not advance easily out of the container, put it briefly in the freezer and then try again.

[61] Instructions from Classic Shaving: See http://tinyurl.com/2abtlr

[62] This excellent tutorial: See http://tinyurl.com/pylqk

[63] Superlather: See http://tinyurl.com/2a2z7t

[64] A comment: See http://tinyurl.com/2a2uuq

[65] Microphotographs: See http://tinyurl.com/3mzl3t

[66] Feather Blade Safe: See http://tinyurl.com/2ddz2k

[67] These at Classic Shaving: See http://tinyurl.com/cdatg

[68] If you're willing to undertake learning to use a straight razor, check out StraightRazorPlace.com and also *The Art of the Straight-Razor Shave,* by Chris Moss—see http://tinyurl.com/2c4zuz. For straight razors—sharpened, honed, and ready to shave—and accessories and advice, contact the highly regarded The Well Shaved Gentleman.

[69] Three types of razors: http://tinyurl.com/yqxeah

[70] A rack: See http://tinyurl.com/4ydk4u

[71] A good review: See http://tinyurl.com/2hgqmh

[72] Edwin Jagger razors: See http://tinyurl.com/22blw6

[73] Loading Progress: See http://tinyurl.com/24cgdb

[74] This advice (Futur): See http://tinyurl.com/2dsrxe

[75] Vision user's manual: See http://tinyurl.com/2b4h5t

[76] Common Gillette razors: See http://tinyurl.com/2zq4yh

[77] Dates of Gillette razors: See http://tinyurl.com/k9g2n

[78] Lady Gillette photos: See http://tinyurl.com/3m5ldg

[79] Schick Injector: See http://tinyurl.com/ygf3mn

[80] GEM G-Bar: See http://tinyurl.com/26mh3z

[81] Schick various models: See http://tinyurl.com/27vor9

[82] Pella injector: See http://www.tedpella.com/dissect_html/dissect.htm#anchor1590232

[83] Pella single-edged blades: See http://www.tedpella.com/dissect_html/dissect.htm#anchor1606431

[84] Clean it: See http://tinyurl.com/yuuuk5

[85] Maas metal polish: See http://tinyurl.com/yph6w3

[86] Shaver noted: See http://tinyurl.com/28g7wj

[87] Ultrasonic cleaner: See http://tinyurl.com/24b6n4

[88] Holding the tip: See http://tinyurl.com/2955zd

[89] Pointed out angle: See http://tinyurl.com/yuz6p4

[90] Tiny travel razor: See http://tinyurl.com/yuuwxn

[91] A similar approach: See http://tinyurl.com/29sstk

[92] Useful diagram: See http://tinyurl.com/ynkb5o

[93] The basic (4-pass) method: See http://tinyurl.com/2akgaq

[94] Advanced shaving techniques: See http://tinyurl.com/2y9ovh

[95] Hydrolast Cutting Balm: See http://tinyurl.com/3ktec2

[96] Total Shaving Solution: See http://tinyurl.com/62nud6

[97] All Natural Shaving Oil: See http://pacificshaving.com/

[98] Kinexium ST Shaving Oil: See http://tinyurl.com/6bmbzc

[99] Gessato Pre-Shave Oil: See http://tinyurl.com/5b9srw

[100] Rituals Skincare Pre-Shave Oil: See http://tinyurl.com/6m7luq

[101] Milk and Honey Lotion: See http://tinyurl.com/6zy28d

[102] Non-comedogenic chart: See http://tinyurl.com/555esn

[103] Natural 1 oz bottle: See http://tinyurl.com/4w8beb

[104] Cobalt blue 1 oz bottle: See http://tinyurl.com/4fbabt

[105] First Method video: See http://tinyurl.com/4llmby

[106] Method shaving supplies: See http://tinyurl.com/3ktec2

[107] Shaver's comment: See http://tinyurl.com/2e2n38

[108] One woman notes: See http://tinyurl.com/yqx6vk

[109] My Nik Is Sealed: See http://tinyurl.com/2hzk8r#sealed

[110] Lengthy review: See http://tinyurl.com/35ekgm

[111] Variety of fragrances: See http://tinyurl.com/y8kw3o

[112] Sampler package: See http://tinyurl.com/265x8v

[113] Thayers Aftershave: See http://tinyurl.com/2c3vnd

[114] An entire array: See http://tinyurl.com/yrpb6e

[115] Booster's aftershaves: See http://tinyurl.com/58ke3u

[116] Proraso pre- and after-shave: See http://tinyurl.com/yr8kn5

[117] Mild acne photos: See http://tinyurl.com/5yy46f

[118] Moderate acne: See http://tinyurl.com/4dw4sf

[119] Severe acne: See http://tinyurl.com/3old4v

[120] Sulfur-based compounds: See http://tinyurl.com/6ef7x6

[121] AcneNet: See http://tinyurl.com/498ksr

[122] Acne.org: See http://www.acne.org/ See also this post for additional tips that may be of help: http://tinyurl.com/6etgup

[123] Low comedogenicity: See http://tinyurl.com/696gsf

[124] Mayo Clinic articles: See http://tinyurl.com/44ufoj

[125] Pictures of razor bumps and rash: See http://tinyurl.com/3qg7bh

[126] Themba's technique: See the threads at http://tinyurl.com/yr5lz6 and http://tinyurl.com/5qbqpj (scroll down at both links)

[127] Innomed Lice Comb: Easily found with a Google search

[128] Moore Unique Razor Bump Tool: See http://tinyurl.com/3q9aam

[129] Bump Fighter Razor: See http://tinyurl.com/59lm8f

[130] Barbicide: http://tinyurl.com/4pvmou

[131] Bump Fighter: See http://tinyurl.com/6fuc4d

Bump Patrol: See http://tinyurl.com/3rt6hu

Dermagen Skin Revival System: See http://tinyurl.com/43v9yw

Elicina Biological Treatment: See http://tinyurl.com/4ampxj

Follique treatment: See http://tinyurl.com/4d25ow

High Time Bump Stopper Products: See http://tinyurl.com/4l82dx

Moore Unique Products: See http://tinyurl.com/44zbya

No Mo' Bumps Aftershave: See http://tinyurl.com/3uugej

Prince Reigns Gel: See http://tinyurl.com/4buq27

Smart Shave Products: See http://tinyurl.com/528cxl

Tend Skin: See http://tinyurl.com/m6o6e

[132] Homemade version of Tend Skin: See http://tinyurl.com/63jsl3

[133] A beginner shaving kit: See http://tinyurl.com/2fao4t

[134] Edwin Jagger razors: See http://tinyurl.com/5ro5sn

[135] Bump Fighter Razor: See http://tinyurl.com/59lm8f

[136] Write-up on MSNBC: See http://tinyurl.com/48evm

[137] "How-to-use" guide: See http://tinyurl.com/2f2wcl

[138] Series of videos: See http://tinyurl.com/y2fx33

[139] A comprehensive list: See http://tinyurl.com/2gwu8c